Italian Cookbook

Traditional Italian Recipes Made Easy

www.grizzlypublishing.com

Table of Contents

Introduction

I want to thank you for choosing this book, *'Italian Cookbook: Traditional Italian Recipes Made Easy.'*

If you were to ask people what's their favorite stress busting activity, more often than not, you would hear 'cooking' as the answer. The best part about cooking is you get to enjoy the results of your hard work almost instantly. The texture of various ingredients, the sound of sizzling and popping when baking or frying, the colors and smells of the food and, of course, the taste of the finished dish - all of these will tantalize your taste buds.

Most people love food and the idea of cooking and are open to experimentation with various cuisines from different parts of the world. Of all the countries and their special cuisine, one country that stands out in the culinary department is Italy. The first thing that comes to mind when we speak of Italy is the delicious and hearty Italian food, which is loved by young and old ones alike across the world.

People often think Italian cooking and cuisine is all about pastas and pizzas and all that goes in an Italian dish are tomatoes, herbs and cheese. Although these ingredients do form a major part of Italian cuisine, it does not revolve around them. There is much more to this glorious cuisine than a cheesy pasta or a hearty pizza.

Although traditional, Italian cooking is quite flexible as well. The dishes are often quite simple and can be cooked with minimal ingredients. These recipes are soft on the palette with a burst of flavors of the prime ingredients. Some of these ingredients are only available in certain seasons and expert cooks know how to and when to use them to make the dishes pop. Italian cuisine is extremely rich and often calls for fresh vegetables and herbs. However, thanks to its flexible nature, it is possible to use canned foods in these traditional recipes too.

Generous use of herbs, vegetables and olive oil makes this cuisine extremely healthy. Italian recipes are so colorful, that your plate will often end up looking like a rainbow. Italian cuisine is often divided into southern cuisine and northern cuisine. Although both of these use almost similar ingredients, the taste can be quite different. The Italian food that is available outside of Italy is often an amalgamation of both these cuisines.

In Italy, each holiday has its own special recipe. These recipes often call for special, seasonal ingredients. Finding these ingredients outside of Italy can be quite difficult. However, you can always replace them with other ingredients to give a new twist to the age-old recipes. Remember, Italian cooking is all about flexibility, experimentation and inclusion.

The intent of this book is to acquaint you with traditional Italian recipes and make Italian cooking easy for novice cooks. The best part about this book is it contains a perfect blend of new and old, traditional and modern, authentic and fusion recipes, making it a perfect read for anyone who wants to taste authentic Italian flavors. The recipes are divided into different sections for the ease of readers. To make it simple for you, optional or alternate ingredients are mentioned next to ingredients difficult to procure in local supermarkets.

The recipes in this book are simple, easy to make and delicious. Anyone with a rudimentary knowledge of cooking can use this book to make delicious Italian delicacies. All the recipes are tried, tested and tasted so you can be rest assured of the final product, as long as you follow the recipes properly.

As said earlier, Italian cooking is all about flexibility so if you do not like a particular ingredient, you can change it or replace with another ingredient, which is similar in texture or taste. To add a fusion twist to the recipes, you can even experiment with ingredients of your choice but, before you do that, try to create the original recipe.

Without any further ado, let us get started. Thank you once again for choosing this book. I sincerely hope you have fun cooking and serving these Italian recipes to your near and dear ones.

Chapter One: Italian Breakfast Recipes

Italian Sausage Egg Bake

Serves: 6

Ingredients:

- 4 slices white bread, cubed
- 1 cup sharp cheddar cheese, shredded
- 5 large eggs, lightly beaten
- ½ teaspoon dried oregano
- ½ teaspoon dried basil
- ½ pound mild Italian sausage links, discard casings, sliced
- 1 cup part skim mozzarella cheese
- 1 ½ cups 2% milk
- ½ teaspoon fennel seeds, crushed

Method:

1. Grease a baking dish and place bread in it.
2. Place a skillet over medium heat. Add sausage and cook until it is not pink anymore. Discard excess fat in the pan.
3. Turn off the heat and spread sausage over the bread cubes.
4. Sprinkle mozzarella cheese and cheddar cheese.
5. Cover with cling wrap and chill for 6-8 hours.
6. Let it sit for 30 minutes. Discard the wrap.
7. Bake in a preheated oven at 350° F for 40-50 minutes or a toothpick, when inserted in the center, comes out clean.

8. Remove from the oven and let it sit for 5 minutes.
9. Slice and serve.

Vegetable Pizza Burritos

Serves: 8

Ingredients:

- 2 cans (15 ounce each) white beans, rinsed, drained
- 2 cans (15 ounces each) diced tomatoes, drained
- 1 cup olives, sliced
- 2 cups green bell pepper, chopped
- 1 large onion, chopped
- 8 flour tortillas
- 2 teaspoons Italian seasoning
- 2 cups cheese of your choice, shredded
- A handful fresh basil, chopped, to garnish

Method:

1. Place a skillet over medium heat. Add oil. When oil is heated, add onions and bell pepper and sauté until translucent.
2. Add tomatoes, beans and Italian seasoning and stir until well combined.
3. Add cheese and olives and mix well. Heat thoroughly.
4. Add basil. Mix well.
5. Divide the filling equally and place over the tortillas. Roll and serve.

Brunch Torte

Serves: 6

Ingredients:

- 1 tube (8 ounces) refrigerated crescent rolls, divided
- 3 ounces baby spinach
- 4 large eggs
- 1 teaspoon Italian seasoning
- ¼ pound deli ham, thinly sliced
- ¼ pound provolone cheese, sliced
- 1 jar (12 ounces each) roasted sweet red peppers, drained, sliced, pat dried
- ½ teaspoon olive oil
- ½ cup fresh mushrooms
- ½ cup parmesan cheese, grated
- Pepper powder to taste
- ¼ pound hard salami, thinly sliced

Method:

1. Grease a small springform pan with oil or butter. Place it on a large sheet of heavy-duty foil. Wrap the foil all around the pan tightly.
2. Unroll half the dough and keep the triangles separately on the prepared pan. Press it well on to the bottom of the pan.
3. Bake in a preheated oven at 350° F for 10-15 minutes.
4. Place a skillet over medium heat. Add oil. When the oil is heated, add spinach and mushrooms and sauté until tender.

5. Remove with a slotted spoon and place on a plate that is lined with paper towels.
6. Add 5 eggs into a bowl and whisk well. Add cheese, pepper and Italian seasoning.
7. Place ham over the crust. Layer with salami and cheese followed by red pepper and spinach mixture.
8. Pour beaten egg on top.
9. Unroll the remaining dough. Place them close to each other and form into a circle. Press them together so that it will not open up.
10. Carefully place it over the filling on the crust.
11. Beat the remaining egg and brush it over the dough.
12. Bake in a preheated oven at 350° F for 40-60 minutes or the internal temperature should show 160 ° F.
13. If you find that the top is browning too quickly, cover with foil and continue baking.
14. Run a knife around the edges of the container. Take off the rim from the springform pan.
15. Let it sit for 20 minutes.
16. Slice and serve.

Italian Scramble

Serves: 6-8

Ingredients:

- 2 packages tofu, crumbled
- 4 cloves garlic, minced or pressed
- 2 medium onions, chopped
- 1 green chili, thinly sliced
- 1 green or red bell pepper, chopped
- 2 tablespoons olive oil
- 2 tablespoons Italian seasoning or to taste
- 1 ½ teaspoons crushed red pepper flakes
- 1 teaspoon turmeric powder
- 2 bunches spinach, rinsed, chopped
- 2 cups cherry tomatoes
- 4 tablespoons capers
- 1 ½ teaspoons sea salt or to taste

Method:

1. Place a skillet over medium heat. Add oil. When oil is heated, add onions and bell peppers and sauté until soft.
2. Add turmeric and Italian seasoning and sauté for a few seconds.
3. Add spinach, green chili and tomatoes and sauté until spinach wilts.
4. Add tofu and capers. Mix well and heat thoroughly. Taste and adjust the seasonings if necessary.
5. Serve hot.

Egg and Tomato Scramble

Serves: 2

Ingredients:

- 2 plum tomatoes, peeled, chopped
- 2 eggs or egg substitute equivalent
- 2 cloves garlic, minced
- Salt to taste
- Pepper to taste
- 1 tablespoon fresh basil or ½ teaspoon dried basil and extra to garnish
- 2 teaspoons water
- 2 teaspoons olive oil (optional)
- 2 slices bread, toasted

Method:

1. Add egg, garlic and water into a bowl and whisk well.
2. Add tomato and basil into another bowl. Mix well.
3. Place a small nonstick skillet over medium heat. Add oil. When the oil is heated, add the egg mixture. Stir and cook until the eggs are soft and nearly set.
4. Stir in the tomato-basil mixture, salt and pepper.
5. Cook until eggs are fully set.
6. Place a toast in each serving plate. Divide the scramble among the plates and serve.

Decadently Thick Italian Hot Chocolate

Serves: 4-8

Ingredients:

- 4 tablespoons butter
- 2 cups chopped chocolate or chocolate chips
- 4 cups milk of your choice
- 4 teaspoons cornstarch
- 4 tablespoons granulated sugar or more to taste
- ½ teaspoon vanilla extract (optional)

Method:

1. Place a saucepan over low heat. Add butter. When butter melts, add cornstarch and mix until well combined.
2. Add milk and sugar and stir. Raise heat to medium high. Bring to a simmer stirring constantly.
3. Lower heat and add chocolate. Simmer until thick and chocolate melts completely.
4. Remove from heat and add vanilla extract.
5. Mix well, pour into cups and serve.

Pizza Omelet

Serves: 2

Ingredients:

- 4 eggs
- 2 tablespoons butter
- 20 slices pepperoni
- ½ cup part skim mozzarella cheese, shredded
- 4 tablespoons milk
- ½ cup pizza sauce
- 2 tablespoons shredded parmesan cheese

Method:

1. Whisk together eggs and milk.
2. Place a small skillet over medium heat.
3. Add half the butter. When butter melts, pour half the egg mixture.
4. Cook until the omelet is set. Carefully slide on to a plate.
5. Spread half the pizza sauce over one half of the omelet. Place half the pepperoni slices and sprinkle half the mozzarella cheese.
6. Fold the other half over the filling. Sprinkle 1-tablespoon Parmesan cheese and serve.
7. Repeat steps 3-6 to make the other omelet.

Brunch Risotto

Serves: 4

Ingredients:

- 2 ½ cups low sodium chicken broth or more if required, warmed
- 1 cup Arborio rice, rinsed
- Pepper powder to taste
- 1 small tomato, chopped
- 6 ounces Italian sausage links, discard casings
- 1 small clove garlic, minced
- ½ tablespoon olive oil

Method:

1. Place a nonstick skillet over medium heat. Add sausage and cook until it is not pink anymore. Discard excess fat in the pan.
2. Place the skillet back over heat. Add oil. When the oil is heated, add garlic, rice and pepper and sauté until rice turns opaque – 2-3 minutes.
3. Add sausage back into the skillet. Add ½ cup of broth and stir. Cook until broth is absorbed.
4. Add ½ cup of broth each time and cook until it is absorbed. Repeat this until all the broth is added. If the rice is not tender, add some more broth.
5. Add tomato and heat thoroughly.
6. Stir right away.

Chocolate-Banana Melts

Serves: 1

Ingredients:

- 1 tablespoon chocolate hazelnut spread like Nutella
- 1 small banana, sliced
- 2 teaspoons dark brown sugar
- 2 slices soft sandwich bread
- A little butter, at room temperature

Method:

1. Spread ½ tablespoon chocolate spread on 1 slice of bread.
2. Place banana slices over it. Cover with the other slice of bread.
3. Brush butter on the topside of the bread.
4. Sprinkle 1-teaspoon sugar over it and press it onto the bread slice.
5. Place a nonstick pan over medium low heat. Place the sandwich on the skillet, the sugar side facing down. Cook until golden brown.
6. Brush the other side with butter and sprinkle remaining sugar over it and press it onto the bread slice.
7. Flip sides and cook the other side too.
8. Cut into the desired shape and serve.

Breakfast Casserole

Serves: 4

Ingredients:

- 2 large egg whites
- 4 large eggs
- 1 tablespoon low fat parmesan cheese, grated
- 1 tablespoon fresh oregano leaves
- ½ teaspoon garlic powder
- 2 cloves garlic, sliced
- 1/3 cup plain almond milk
- 2 tablespoons feta cheese, crumbled
- ½ teaspoon paprika
- ¼ teaspoon freshly ground black pepper
- 2 ounces baby spinach
- 2 canned artichoke hearts in water, chopped
- ½ cup mushrooms, sliced
- 2 green onions, sliced
- Salt to taste

Method:

1. Add eggs, whites, oregano, Parmesan, feta cheese, garlic powder, milk, salt and pepper to a large bowl. Mix until well combined.
2. Grease a baking dish with a little oil or butter.
3. Layer the spinach, tomatoes, artichoke, garlic, green onion and mushrooms in the baking dish.
4. Pour the egg mixture on top. Fold lightly.
5. Bake in a preheated oven at 350° F for 20-30 minutes or until set.
6. Remove from the oven and let it rest for 10 minutes.

7. Slice and serve.

Ham and Egg Breakfast Casserole

Serves: 12

Ingredients:

- ½ pound fresh mushrooms, coarsely chopped
- ½ teaspoon Italian seasoning
- 2 cups sharp Cheddar cheese, shredded
- ¼ cup parmesan cheese, shredded
- 12 large eggs
- ½ tablespoon Dijon mustard
- 3 tablespoons butter, cubed
- Black pepper powder to taste
- 1 cup cooked ham, cubed
- 1 tablespoon all-purpose flour
- 1 cup heavy whipping cream
- White pepper powder to taste

Method:

1. Place a skillet over medium heat. Add butter. When butter melts, add mushrooms and sauté until slightly tender.
2. Stir in black pepper and Italian seasoning. Mix well and turn off the heat.
3. Transfer into a greased baking dish.
4. Add ham, Cheddar cheese, flour and Parmesan cheese into a bowl. Mix well.
5. Spread over the mushrooms in the baking dish.
6. Add eggs, white pepper, mustard and cream into a bowl and whisk well. Pour into the baking dish.
7. Cover with foil and chill or freeze until use. It can be frozen for 3 months.

8. Bake in a preheated oven at 350° F for 30-40 minutes or until set. A toothpick, when inserted in the center, should come out clean.
9. Remove from the oven and let it sit for 10 minutes.
10. Slice and serve.

Italian Breakfast Potato and Ham Casserole

Serves: 8

Ingredients:

- 8 medium red potatoes, sliced
- 16 eggs, lightly beaten
- 4 cups spaghetti sauce
- 4 tablespoons vegetable oil
- 2 tablespoons butter
- 1 cup cheddar cheese, shredded
- 1 cup mozzarella cheese, shredded
- 1 pound thinly sliced, fully cooked ham, diced

Method:

1. Place a skillet over medium heat. Add oil. When the oil is heated, add potatoes and cook until tender.
2. Remove the potatoes with a slotted spoon and divide into 8 ovenproof containers (16 ounces each).
3. Place the skillet back over heat. Add butter. When butter melts, add eggs and stir. Cook until the eggs are set and scrambled.
4. Divide the scrambled eggs among the containers. Divide the ham and place over the eggs.
5. Add half-cup spaghetti sauce into each container. Divide the cheese among the containers.
6. Bake in a preheated oven at 350° F for 30-40 minutes or until cheese melts and the casserole is bubbling. Bake in batches.

Sausage 'n' Spinach Eggs

Serves: 4

Ingredients:

- ½ pound Johnsonville Ground hot Italian sausage
- ¼ pound fresh mushrooms, sliced
- Salt to taste
- Pepper to taste
- 1/8 teaspoon dried oregano
- 4 cups fresh spinach, torn
- A dash hot pepper sauce
- 1 large onion, finely chopped
- 4 cloves garlic, minced
- 1/8 teaspoon ground nutmeg
- 1 tablespoon olive oil
- 4 large eggs
- ½ cup Monterey Jack cheese, shredded

Method:

1. Place an ovenproof skillet over medium heat. Add sausage. Cook until it is not pink anymore. Break it simultaneously as it cooks.
2. Remove sausage with a slotted spoon and set aside.
3. Drain the fat remaining in the skillet. Add oil. When the oil is heated, add onion, garlic, mushrooms, nutmeg, oregano, salt and pepper and sauté until tender.
4. Stir in the spinach and sauté until spinach wilts.
5. Meanwhile, add eggs and hot pepper sauce into a bowl and whisk well.

6. Add the sausage back into the skillet. Pour eggs into skillet. Do not stir. Let the eggs set slightly. Lift the edges of the mixture so that the egg goes down below.
7. Turn off the heat and transfer the skillet into a preheated broiler.
8. Broil for a few minutes until the egg sets.
9. Sprinkle cheese on top. Broil for a couple of minutes more or until cheese melts.
10. Slice into wedges and serve.

Three-Cheese Quiche

Serves: 12

Ingredients:

- 10 large egg yolks
- 14 large eggs
- 2 cups heavy whipping cream
- 2 cups part- skim mozzarella cheese, shredded
- 1 cup Swiss cheese
- 3 teaspoons salt free seasoning blend
- 2 cups half and half cream
- 1 ½ cups sharp cheddar cheese, divided
- 4 tablespoons finely chopped oil-packed, sun dried tomatoes
- ½ teaspoon dried basil

Method:

1. Set aside ½ cup cheddar cheese and add rest of the ingredients into a bowl and mix until well combined.
2. Divide the mixture into 2 deep-dish pie plates that is greased with a little butter or oil.
3. Sprinkle the cheddar cheese that was set aside.
4. Bake in a preheated oven at 350° F for 45-50 minutes or a toothpick when inserted in the center of the quiche should come out clean. Bake in batches.
5. Remove from the oven and cool for 10 minutes. Slice and serve.

Italian Easter Bread Breakfast Casserole

Serves: 4

Ingredients:

For casserole:

- 2 cups Colomba medium cubed or any other sweet bread of your choice
- 2 small eggs
- 1 tablespoon brown sugar
- 1/8 teaspoon salt
- 1 tablespoon butter, melted,
- ½ cup + 2 tablespoons milk
- 1 teaspoon ground cinnamon

For topping:

- 1 teaspoon ground cinnamon
- 1 ½ tablespoons flour
- 2 tablespoons brown sugar
- 1 ½ tablespoons butter

To serve: Use any, as required

- Maple syrup
- Powdered sugar

Method:

1. For the casserole. Add eggs and milk into a bowl and whisk well. Add cinnamon, salt and brown sugar and whisk until well combined.

2. Pour butter into a small casserole dish. Spread the bread cubes in the dish. Pour the egg mixture over it. Mix gently until well combined. Let it soak for a while.

3. For topping: Add flour, brown sugar and cinnamon into a small bowl. Add butter and cut it into the mixture. Mix until tiny crumbs are formed.

4. Sprinkle this mixture over the bread.

5. Bake in a preheated oven at 350° F for 45-50 minutes or until cooked through.

6. Let it rest for a few minutes.

7. Cut into slices and serve with maple syrup or powdered sugar.

Frutti di Bosco, Oat & Almond Smoothie

Serves: 2

Ingredients:

- ½ cup frutti di bosco (mixed berries), fresh or frozen
- 4 tablespoons old fashioned oats
- 2 cups almond milk or regular milk
- Lingonberry concentrate or honey to taste

Method:

1. Add oats into a blender and blend until finely powdered.
2. Add berries, milk and sweetener and blend again until well combined and smooth.
3. Pour into glasses and serve.

Chapter Two: Italian Lunch Recipes

Italian Fruit Shake (Frullato)

Serves: 2

Ingredients:

- ½ red apple, peeled, cored, chopped
- 1 small banana, sliced
- 1 apricot, deseeded, chopped
- ½ pear or peach, peeled, chopped
- ½ orange, peeled, separated into segments, deseeded
- 2 cups milk
- Sugar to taste
- Ice cubes, as required

Method:

1. Add milk, apple, pear, banana and orange into a blender.
2. Blend until smooth.
3. Pour into tall chilled glasses and serve.

Pineapple – Banana Frullato

Serves: 2

Ingredients:

- 2 slices pineapple
- Juice of ½ lemon
- Juice of an orange
- 1 ½ bananas, peeled, sliced
- ¼ cup chilled sugar syrup

Method:

1. Add pineapple, banana, sugar syrup, lemon juice and orange juice into a blender.
2. Blend until smooth.
3. Pour into tall chilled glasses and serve garnished with an orange slice or lemon slice.

Melon Frullato

Serves: 2

Ingredients:

- ½ melon (honeydew or watermelon or cantaloupe), peeled, cubed, deseeded
- Juice of ½ lemon
- 2 teaspoons sugar
- 1 teaspoon liquor of your choice (optional)
- Ice cubes, as required
- 2 cups dry Chablis

Method:

1. Add melon, lemon juice, sugar, liquor, ice cubes and Chablis into a blender.
2. Blend until smooth.
3. Pour into tall chilled glasses and serve garnished with a melon slice.

Quick Italian Pasta Salad

Serves: 6

Ingredients:

- 6 ounces tri-color rotini pasta, cook according to instructions on the package
- 1 small red bell pepper, sliced
- 1 small green bell pepper, sliced
- 6 ounces Italian salami, finely chopped
- 1 medium red onion, chopped
- 3 ounces canned sliced black olives
- 8 tablespoons Italian style salad dressing
- 1 ½ packages (0.7 ounces each) dry Italian style salad dressing mix or to taste
- 4 ounces small fresh mozzarella balls (ciliegine)
- ¼ cup parmesan cheese, shredded

Method:

1. Add all the ingredients except dry salad dressing and Parmesan cheese into a bowl and toss well.
2. Add dry dressing and toss again. Taste and add more dressing if necessary.
3. Sprinkle Parmesan cheese.
4. Chill for a while if desired and serve.

Big Italian salad

Serves: 8-10

Ingredients:

For the dressing:

- 2 cups fresh Italian parsley, loosely packed
- ½ teaspoon dried oregano
- ½ cup red wine vinegar
- 1 cup extra virgin olive oil
- ½ teaspoon pepper
- 3 teaspoons honey
- 20-25 big leaves of basil
- 4 cloves garlic, peeled
- 1 ½ teaspoon salt or to taste

For salad:

- 2 large heads romaine lettuce, washed, chopped
- ½ cup green olives, pitted
- 2 cups hothouse cucumber, sliced
- 1 cup cherry tomatoes or grape tomatoes, halved
- 2 large bell peppers, chopped
- 2 large carrots, halved, thinly sliced
- 1 cup ricotta

Method:

1. Mix together all the ingredients of the salad in a large bowl.
2. Add all the ingredients of the dressing into a blender and blend until smooth.

3. Pour about half the dressing over the salad and toss well.
4. Taste and add more dressing if required.

Ultimate Caprese Salad

Serves: 2

Ingredients:

- ½ pint mixed cherry tomatoes, preferably heirloom tomatoes, halved
- Flaky sea salt to taste
- 4 ounces buffalo mozzarella or mozzarella cheese, at room temperature, torn into pieces
- A handful small basil leaves
- 3 ½ tablespoons extra-virgin olive oil, divided
- 1 pound mixed medium and large tomatoes, preferably heirloom, thinly sliced or cut into wedges
- Coarsely ground pepper to taste
- Country bread slices, toasted, to serve

Method:

1. Add cherry tomatoes, salt and ½ tablespoon oil into a bowl and toss well.
2. Place tomato slices, slightly overlapping each other on a serving platter. Sprinkle a generous amount of salt.
3. Place mozzarella cheese over the tomatoes. Sprinkle salt over the cheese.
4. Spread the cherry tomatoes over the salad. Drizzle remaining oil. Sprinkle pepper.
5. Set aside for a while for the flavors to set in.
6. Garnish with basil and serve with country bread slices.

Italian Crudités

Serves: 4

Ingredients:

- 4 small carrots, halved
- 4 thin asparagus spears, trimmed
- 1 cup broccoli florets or cauliflower florets
- 1 endive, leaves separated
- 2 spring onions, trimmed, halved
- 1 ounce haricot verts, trimmed
- Flaky sea salt to taste
- 4 red radishes, trimmed, thinly sliced
- ½ celery heart, cut into 4 wedges
- 1 small fennel bulbs, halved
- 1 head Little Gem lettuce, leaves separated
- ¼ bunch watercress, tough stem removed
- Lemon juice, as required
- ½ cup olive oil

Method:

1. Decorate all the vegetables on a large serving platter in any manner you desire.
2. Drizzle lemon juice all over. Season with salt.
3. Divide the oil in 4 small bowls, for dipping. Serve salad with oil.

Radicchio, Fennel, and Olive Panzanella

Serves: 2

Ingredients:

For dressing:

- 2 tablespoons olive oil
- 2 tablespoons finely chopped shallot
- ½ tablespoon fresh oregano, chopped
- 1 tablespoon red wine vinegar
- 1 tablespoon fresh lemon juice
- Salt to taste

For salad:

- 2 ounces local bread, cut into small pieces (about 2 cups)
- 2 tablespoons olive oil
- ½ small head radicchio, torn into bite size pieces
- ½ cup fresh parsley leaves, chopped
- 1.5 ounces aged sheep milk cheese like Manchego, shaved
- ½ small fennel bulb, thinly sliced
- ¼ cup green olive, pitted, halved
- 1.5 ounces hard salami, thinly sliced
- ½ teaspoon lemon zest, freshly grated

Method:

1. To make dressing: Add all the ingredients of dressing into a small bowl and whisk well. Cover and set aside for a while for the flavors to set in.

2. Meanwhile, add bread, lemon zest and 2 tablespoons oil into a bowl and toss well. Sprinkle salt and pepper.
3. Spread on a rimmed baking sheet.
4. Bake in a preheated oven at 400° F for 8-10 minutes or until crisp on the top. Cool completely.
5. Add all the salad ingredients into a bowl and toss well. Add bread and toss well.
6. Pour dressing on top. Toss well.
7. Chill if desired or serve immediately.

Ratatouille Frittata

Serves: 8

Ingredients:

- 4 cups frozen cubed hash brown potatoes
- 4 Italian sausage links, cooked, diced
- 12 eggs
- ½ teaspoon salt
- 4 tablespoons olive oil
- 4 cups cooked ratatouille
- ½ cup milk
- ¼ teaspoon pepper powder

Method:

1. Place an ovenproof skillet over medium heat.
2. Add oil. When the oil is heated, add hash browns. Cook until brown.
3. Add sausage and ratatouille. Mix well.
4. Add eggs, salt, pepper and milk into a bowl and whisk well.
5. Pour all over the hash brown mixture. Do not stir. Cover with a lid.
6. Lower the heat and cook until it is almost set.
7. Remove the lid of the skillet and broil for a few minutes until it is light brown.

Eggs with Polenta & Pancetta

Serves: 2

Ingredients:

- ¼ cup quick cooking polenta
- 1 ¼ cups water
- 1 ½ tablespoons butter
- 2 eggs
- Toast to serve, as required
- Salt to taste
- Pepper to taste
- 3 tablespoons grated parmesan cheese
- 2 scallions, sliced
- 4 slices pancetta, cooked

Method:

1. Add water and about ¼ teaspoon water into a saucepan. Place saucepan over medium heat.
2. When it begins to boil, add polenta and whisk well.
3. Reduce heat to medium low. Stir constantly until the mixture thickens.
4. Add cheese and ½ tablespoon butter. Sprinkle salt and pepper and mix well. Turn off the heat.
5. Place a skillet over medium heat. Add remaining butter. When butter melts, add scallions and sauté for 30 seconds.
6. Add eggs, salt and pepper. Do not stir. Let the eggs cook to the consistency you desire.
7. Serve polenta into serving bowls. Place eggs pm top. Place pancetta and serve along with toast.

Pasta Frittata

Serves: 3

Ingredients:

- 1 medium onion, chopped
- 6 ounces sliced deli ham, finely chopped
- 2 egg whites
- 3 eggs
- ¼ cup mozzarella cheese, shredded
- 1 teaspoon Italian seasoning
- ¼ teaspoon pepper powder
- 1 cup cooked angel hair pasta
- ½ tablespoon vegetable oil
- 2 cloves garlic, minced
- 1 tablespoon mozzarella cheese, shredded
- ¼ teaspoon salt or to taste

Method:

1. Place an ovenproof skillet over medium heat.
2. Add oil. When the oil is heated, add garlic and ham and sauté for a minute. Remove with a slotted spoon and set aside in a bowl.
3. Add egg whites and eggs into a bowl and whisk well. Stir in the cheese, parsley, pepper, salt and Italian seasoning. Add ham and pasta and mix well.
4. Place the skillet back over medium heat. Transfer the pasta mixture into the skillet. Cover with a lid.
5. Cook for 4 minutes. Turn off the heat.
6. Transfer the skillet into an oven.

7. Bake in a preheated oven at 400° F for 13-15 minutes or until set. A toothpick, when inserted in the center, should come out clean.
8. Let it sit for 5 minutes. Slice and serve.

Vegetarian Egg Strata

Serves: 6

Ingredients:

- 1 small zucchini, finely chopped
- ½ cu baby Portobello mushrooms, sliced
- 1 teaspoon olive oil
- 1 teaspoon fresh thyme, minced or ¼ teaspoon dried thyme
- Pepper to taste
- Salt to taste
- 1 package (5.3 ounces) fresh goat's cheese, crumbled
- 3 eggs, lightly beaten
- 1/8 teaspoon ground nutmeg
- 1 small sweet red pepper, finely chopped
- 1 small red onion, finely chopped
- 2 cloves garlic, minced
- ½ loaf (½ pound) day old French bread, cubed
- 1 cup parmesan cheese, grated
- 1 cup fat free milk

Method:

1. Place a skillet over medium heat. Add oil. When the oil is heated, add zucchini, mushrooms, red pepper and onion. Sauté until slightly soft.
2. Stir in garlic, salt, pepper and thyme. Stir until fragrant.
3. Grease a baking dish with a little oil.
4. Spread the bread cubes in the baking dish.

5. Layer with bread cubes followed by zucchini – mushroom mixture. Sprinkle goat's cheese and Parmesan cheese.
6. Add eggs, nutmeg and milk into a bowl and whisk well. Pour over the cheese layer.
7. Cover with foil and chill for 6-8 hours.
8. Let it sit on the countertop for 30 minutes before baking.
9. Bake in a preheated oven at 400° F for 13-15 minutes or until set. A toothpick, when inserted in the center, should come out clean.
10. Let it sit for 5 minutes. Slice and serve preferably with tomato bisque.

Zuppa Vegana: Italian Kale, Potato and Bean Soup

Serves: 3

Ingredients:

- 1 cup onions, chopped
- ½ pound small potatoes, chopped into bite sized pieces
- 4-6 cups kale leaves, discard hard stems and ribs, chopped
- 4 cloves garlic, minced
- 1 can (15 ounces) pinto beans, drained, rinsed
- 4 cups vegetable broth
- ½ teaspoon dried basil
- ½ teaspoon dried oregano
- ¼ teaspoon dried rosemary, crushed or fresh rosemary sprig
- ¼ teaspoons red pepper flakes
- ¼ teaspoon fennel seeds
- ¼ cup nondairy milk (optional)
- 1 tablespoon nutritional yeast (optional)

Method:

1. Place a soup pot over medium heat. Add onions and a tablespoon of water and sauté until onions turn soft. Add garlic and sauté for a minute.
2. Add rest of the ingredients except kale, milk and nutritional yeast.
3. When it begins to boil, lower the heat and cover with a lid.
4. Cook until the potatoes are tender.

5. Add kale, cover, and cook for 5-8 minutes until kale turn bright green and tender as well.
6. Remove about half the soup and blend in a blender until smooth and pour it back to the pot.
7. Heat thoroughly. Taste and adjust the seasonings if necessary.
8. Add milk and nutritional yeast. Mix well. Discard rosemary sprig.
9. Ladle into soup bowls and serve.

Vegetarian Sausage and Gnocchi Soup

Serves: 3

Ingredients:

- 3 vegetarian sausages, sliced
- 5 ounces gnocchi
- 1 carrot, peeled, chopped
- 1 small onion, chopped
- 1 celery rib, chopped
- 2 cups spinach, chopped
- 1 cup mushrooms, sliced
- 10 ounces canned diced tomatoes with Italian seasoning
- 2 cups vegetable broth
- Freshly ground black pepper to taste
- Salt to taste
- ½ teaspoon Italian seasoning or to taste

To serve:

- Handful fresh parsley, chopped
- Parmesan cheese, grated, as required

Method:

1. Add all the ingredients except spinach and gnocchi into a soup pot. Place the soup pot over medium heat.
2. Cover and cook until the vegetables are nearly tender.
3. Add gnocchi and spinach and cook for a few minutes until done.
4. Ladle into soup bowls. Garnish with Parmesan cheese and parsley and serve.

Italian Subs

Serves: 8

Ingredients:

- 1 large onion, thinly sliced
- 10 tablespoons red wine vinegar
- Salt to taste
- Freshly ground pepper to taste
- ½ pound Genoa salami
- ½ pound deli sliced Capicola
- ½ -1 cup sliced pickled pepperoncini (optional)
- 3 teaspoons dried oregano
- 2 loaves soft Italian bread (12 inches each)
- 10 tablespoons extra-virgin olive oil
- ½ pound deli sliced provolone cheese
- ½ pound deli sliced boiled ham
- 1 head iceberg lettuce, finely shredded
- ½ pound deli sliced mortadella
- 6 plum tomatoes, thinly sliced

Method:

1. Place onions in a bowl of cold water for about 15 minutes and drain.
2. Halve the bread lengthwise and scoop some bread from the inside of the halved bread.
3. Trickle 2 tablespoons oil on the bottom half of each loaf.
4. Trickle 2 tablespoons vinegar on the bottom half of each loaf.
5. Sprinkle salt and pepper over it.

6. Place cheese and salami over it. Place onions over it. Layer with lettuce followed by pepperoncini and tomatoes.
7. Trickle 2 tablespoons of vinegar and 2 tablespoons olive oil over it. Scatter oregano.
8. Sprinkle salt and pepper.
9. Trickle remaining oil and vinegar on the cut part of the top of the loaves.
10. Cover the sandwiches with the top half of the loaves.
11. Cut each sandwich into 4 and serve.

Sriracha BBQ Tofu Pizza with Pepper Jack on Spelt Crust

Serves: 2

Ingredients:

For no rise spelt crust:

- ¾ cup warm water
- 4 teaspoons active yeast
- 2/3 teaspoon salt
- 1 ½ cups spelt flour
- 4 teaspoons extra virgin olive oil
- 2 teaspoons maple syrup
- 2 tablespoons cornstarch or arrowroot starch

For BBQ tofu:

- 4 tablespoons BBQ sauce
- 1 teaspoon garlic powder or paste
- 5-6 teaspoons Sriracha sauce or any other hot sauce
- 2 cups firm tofu, pressed, cubed

Other toppings:

- 1 onion, halved, sliced
- Marinara sauce as required
- 1 bell pepper, sliced
- 1 cup almond milk pepper Jack cheese, shredded
- 2 tablespoons cilantro, chopped

Method:

1. For BBQ tofu: Place the tofu in between kitchen towels. Place something heavy over it for 15 minutes.
2. Add tofu, BBQ sauce, Sriracha sauce and garlic into a bowl and mix well. Let it marinate until use.
3. Meanwhile make spelt crust as follows: Add water, yeast and maple syrup into a large bowl and stir. Set aside for 5-7 minutes or until it becomes frothy.
4. Mix together in another bowl, spelt flour, cornstarch and salt.
5. Add the dry ingredient mixture into the frothy mixture. Add oil and knead until you get smooth dough.
6. Divide the dough into 2 equal portions. Shape into balls.
7. Place on a parchment paper and roll the dough into 2 ovals of about 12 inches size. Place on a baking sheet. Leave it at a warm place for about 10 minutes.
8. Spread marinara sauce over the rolled dough. Scatter the onions and peppers over it. Season with salt and pepper.
9. Layer with tofu pieces. Pour the remaining marinade over it. Sprinkle cheese on top.
10. Bake in a preheated oven at 450 ° F for about 12-13 minutes. Remove from oven.
11. Garnish with cilantro and serve.

Cacio e Pepe

Serves: 3-4

Ingredients:

- 12 ounces pasta egg tagliolini or bucatini spaghetti
- Freshly cracked pepper to taste
- 2/3 cup Pecorino, finely grated
- 1 ½ cups Grana Padano or parmesan cheese, finely grated
- 6 tablespoons unsalted butter, cubed, divided
- Kosher salt to taste

Method:

1. Cook the pasta following the instructions on the package but drain the water 2 minutes before the time mentioned on the package. Retain some of the cooked water (about 2 cups).
2. Place a large heavy bottom skillet over medium heat. Add 4 tablespoons butter. When butter melts, add pepper and toast lightly.
3. Add about a cup of the retained water. When the water begins to boil, add pasta and 2 tablespoons butter.
4. Lower the heat and add Grana Padano cheese. Stir and toss using tongs. When the cheese melts, turn off the heat.
5. Stir in the Pecorino and toss until the cheese melts completely and the pasta is cooked. Add more of the retained water if the sauce is too thick.
6. Spoon into warmed bowls and serve.

Vegetable and Cheese Hoagies

Serves: 2

Ingredients:

- 1 very small red onion, thinly sliced, separated into rings
- 1 small tomato, deseeded, chopped
- ½ tablespoon extra-virgin olive oil
- 1 baguette (8-10 inches long), preferably whole grain
- 1 cup romaine lettuce, shredded
- 7 ounces canned artichoke hearts, rinsed, chopped
- 1 tablespoon balsamic vinegar
- ½ teaspoon dried oregano
- 1 slice provolone cheese (about 1 ounce), halved
- 1/8 cup sliced pepperoncini (optional)

Method:

1. Add onions rings into a bowl of cold water. Set aside for a while. Drain and dry with paper towels.
2. Add artichoke hearts, oregano, vinegar, tomato and oil into a bowl. Toss until well combined.
3. Halve the baguettes lengthwise into 2 equal portions. Carefully scoop out a little of the bread from each half of the baguette.
4. To serve: Place cheese on the bottom half of the baguette. Place artichoke mixture on it. Spread it evenly.
5. Place onion rings, lettuce and pepperoncini. Cover with the top half of the baguette. Chop into 2 halves and serve.

Pasta e Fagioli with Escarole

Serves: 2-3

Ingredients:

- ¾ cup dried cannellini beans, soaked in water overnight
- 1 medium carrot, scrubbed, cut into 2 halves crosswise
- ½ head garlic, halved crosswise
- 1 clove garlic, chopped
- 1 small sprig rosemary
- ¼ teaspoon crushed red pepper flakes + extra for garnishing
- 1 ½ tablespoons olive oil + extra to drizzle
- 7.2 ounces canned peeled whole tomatoes
- 1.5 ounces dried lasagna or any other flat pasta, broken into 1 inch pieces
- ½ parmesan rind (about 1 ounce)
- Shaved parmesan cheese, to serve
- 1 celery stalk, halved crosswise
- 3 sprigs parsley
- 1 bay leaf
- Kosher salt to taste
- Freshly ground pepper to taste
- 1 medium onion, chopped
- 6 tablespoons dry white wine
- ¼ small head escarole, torn into 2 inch pieces
- 1 quart water or more if required

Method:

1. Add Parmesan rind, beans, carrots, ½ head garlic, bay leaves, water, celery, herbs and chilies into a soup pot.
2. Place the pot over medium heat. When the water begins to boil, lower the heat and cover with a lid. Cook until the beans are soft. It may take a couple of hours.
3. Add salt and pepper and stir. Turn off the heat. Let the soup rest for 30 minutes.
4. Remove vegetables, rind and herbs with a slotted spoon and discard.
5. Place a pot over medium heat. Add oil. When the oil is heated, add onions and garlic and sauté until onions are translucent.
6. Crush the tomatoes with your hands and add into the pot. Stir frequently until the liquid in the soup pot is dry.
7. Stir in the wine. Cook until nearly dry.
8. Stir in the beans with the cooked liquid. Simmer until the beans are well blended.
9. Stir in the pasta. Add more water if required. Cook until the pasta is al dente. Add more water if required.
10. Add escarole and cook until it wilts. Add salt and pepper.
11. Divide into soup bowls. Drizzle oil on top. Sprinkle Parmesan cheese and chili flakes on top and serve.

Chapter Three: Italian Dinner Recipes

Tortellini Soup with Sausage

Serves: 4-5

Ingredients:

- ½ pound ground sweet Italian sausage
- 1 stalk celery, chopped
- 1 carrot, chopped
- 1 medium onion, chopped
- 1 ½ cups lacinato kale, discard hard ribs and stems, chopped
- 2 cloves garlic, minced
- Freshly ground black pepper to taste
- Salt to taste
- 3 tablespoons dry white wine or sherry
- 7.5 ounces canned, diced tomatoes
- 4 cups chicken stock
- ½ pound fresh 3 cheese tortellini
- ½ teaspoon dried oregano
- ½ teaspoon dried basil
- ½ teaspoon dried parsley
- Parmesan cheese, grated to garnish

Method:

1. Place a soup pot over medium heat. Add sausage and cook until brown. Break it simultaneously as it cooks.
2. Add celery and onion and sauté for 3-4 minutes. Add garlic and sauté for a few seconds until fragrant.
3. Add salt, pepper and sherry. Scrape the bottom of the pot to remove any browned bits that are stuck.

4. Add rest of the ingredients except tortellini and kale and stir.
5. Cover and lower the heat. Cook for 5-6 minutes.
6. Add tortellini and kale. Cook until tender.
7. Ladle into soup bowls. Garnish with Parmesan cheese and serve.

Italian Wedding Soup

Serves: 4

Ingredients:

- ½ cup white or yellow onions, finely chopped
- 12 small vegan meatballs
- 2 tablespoons olive oil, divided
- 1 medium carrot, chopped
- 2 stalks celery, chopped
- 1 whole clove garlic, peeled, crushed
- 1 teaspoon garlic, minced
- 1/3 cup ditalini pasta
- 2.5 ounces fresh spinach, chopped
- 4 cups vegetable broth
- ½ tablespoon dried oregano
- ½ tablespoon dried parsley
- ½ tablespoon dried basil
- 1 tablespoon lemon juice
- Salt to taste
- Pepper to taste

Method:

1. Place a soup pot over medium heat. Add a tablespoon of oil. When oil is heated, add onions and garlic and sauté until translucent.
2. Add carrots and celery and sauté for 4-5 minutes. Add dried herbs and sauté for a few seconds until fragrant. Add pasta and stir.

3. Lower the heat and simmer for 10 minutes. Add meatballs into the pot and continue simmering for 10 minutes.
4. Meanwhile, place a skillet over medium heat. Add a tablespoon of oil. When oil is heated, add whole clove garlic and cook until light brown. Add spinach and cook until spinach wilts. Transfer into the pot. Add lemon juice, salt and pepper and heat thoroughly.
5. Ladle into soup bowls and serve.

Cioppino

Serves: 3-4

Ingredients:

For broth:
- 1 tablespoon olive oil
- 2 cloves garlic, chopped
- ½ teaspoon dried oregano
- ½ teaspoon dried basil
- 8 ounces clam juice
- ½ can (from a 28 ounces) can whole peeled tomatoes with its liquid
- 1 bay leaf
- 2 parsley sprigs
- ¼ teaspoon crushed red pepper
- Salt to taste
- Freshly ground pepper to taste
- ½ cup dry white wine
- 1 medium onion, chopped

For soup:
- ½ pound white fish fillets, cut into 1 inch pieces
- 1 pound mix mussels (debearded) or clams or cockles, scrubbed
- ½ pound raw large shrimp, peeled, deveined
- 1 tablespoon olive oil
- 1 clove garlic, thinly sliced
- 1 small shallot, finely chopped
- 2 tablespoons unsalted butter, cut into ½ inch cubes
- 2 tablespoons white wine
- ½ tablespoon red wine vinegar (optional)

- 1 teaspoon Italian seasoning
- ¼ teaspoon sugar (optional)
- Salt to taste
- Freshly ground pepper to taste
- Toasted country bread, rubbed with garlic and olive oil, to serve

Method:
1. To make broth: Place a heavy pot over medium heat. Add oil. When the oil is heated, add onions and sauté until translucent.
2. Stir in the garlic, red pepper flakes, oregano and basil. Sauté for a couple of minutes until aromatic.
3. Lower the heat and stir in the wine. Raise the heat to high heat. Boil until the wine is reduced to half its original quantity.
4. Crush the tomatoes with your hands and add into the pot. Cook until thick. Stir occasionally.
5. Add bay leaf, parsley sprigs, 4 cups water, clam juice, salt and pepper. When it begins to boil, lower the heat and simmer for 10-15 minutes. Remove the parsley sprig and bay leaf and discard it.
6. The broth can be made a couple of days in advance and chilled until use.
7. To make soup: Place a heavy soup pot over medium heat. Add oil. When the oil is heated, add shallot and sauté until translucent.
8. Add garlic and sauté for a minute until aromatic. Turn off the heat and stir in the wine and mussels.
9. Place the pot over medium high heat. Cover with lid. In a while the shells will open up. Discard the mussels that do not open. It should take 4-5 minutes. Stir occasionally.

10. Add the cooked broth. When it begins to boil, add shrimp and fish. Cover with a lid. Cook until the fish turns opaque.
11. Add butter, salt and pepper and stir.
12. Ladle into soup bowls. Sprinkle parsley on top and serve with toasted country bread.

Italian Vegetable Stew

Serves: 3-4

Ingredients:

- 3 cups sourdough bread, cut into 2 inch pieces
- ½ bunch Tuscan or other cake, discard central ribs and stems
- ¼ cup olive oil, divided + extra to serve
- 1 stalk celery, finely chopped
- 2 cloves garlic, chopped
- ½ can (from a 28 ounces can) whole peeled tomatoes, drained
- 1 ½ cans (15 ounces each) cannellini beans, rinsed
- 1 sprig marjoram or oregano
- Freshly ground pepper to taste
- Salt to taste
- ½ bunch collard greens, discard central ribs and stems
- ¼ cup olive oil, divided, + extra to serve
- 2 cloves garlic, chopped
- 4 cups low sodium vegetable broth
- ¼ teaspoon crushed red pepper flakes
- 2 sprigs thyme
- 1 bay leaf
- 1 small leek, white and pale green parts only
- Shaved parmesan cheese, to serve

Method:

1. Spread the bread pieces on a rimmed baking sheet. Set aside at room temperature for at least 2 hours.

2. Place a large pot over medium heat. Pour 6-7 cups water. Add a little salt.
3. When the water begins to boil, add collard greens and cook for 2-3 minutes until it wilts. Remove with a slotted spoon and place in a bowl. Rinse in cold water and drain.
4. Add kale into the simmering water and cook for 2-3 minutes until it wilts. Remove with a slotted spoon and place in another bowl. Rinse in cold water and drain.
5. Squeeze the kale and collard greens of excess moisture.
6. Place a heavy bottom pot over medium heat. Add 2 tablespoons oil. When the oil is heated, add carrots, leek and celery. Sauté until tender.
7. Stir in the garlic and red pepper flakes. Sauté for a few seconds until aromatic.
8. Crush the tomatoes using your hands and add into the pot. Sauté for a few minutes until thick. Stir frequently.
9. Stir in the broth, beans, salt, pepper, herbs, bay leaf, kale and collard greens. When it begins to boil, lower the heat and simmer until the soup thickens according to the way you like.
10. Remove the thyme sprig and bay leaf.
11. Add bread pieces and 2 tablespoons oil into the pot and stir.
12. Ladle into soup bowls. Sprinkle Parmesan cheese on top. Drizzle some oil if desired and serve.

Sausage and Broccoli Rabe Frittata

Serves: 4

Ingredients:

- 6 large eggs
- ½ bunch broccoli rabe, coarsely chopped
- 6 tablespoons cheddar cheese, grated, divided
- 1 tablespoon vegetable oil
- ¼ pound chorizo (Spanish or Italian sausage will do) remove the links and casing
- ¼ cup whole milk
- Salt to taste
- Coarsely ground pepper to taste
- 1 small onion, chopped

Method:

1. Add eggs and milk into a bowl and whisk well. Add 3 tablespoons cheddar, salt and pepper and stir. Set aside.
2. Place a cast iron skillet over medium heat. Add chorizo and onions and sauté until chorizo is brown.
3. Stir in broccoli rabe, salt and pepper and sauté until tender. Stir occasionally.
4. Lower the heat to low heat. Add the egg mixture over the chorizo mixture. Cook until the edges are set. Shake the skillet a couple of times while it is cooking.
5. Sprinkle remaining cheddar cheese on top.
6. Transfer the skillet into a preheated oven. Broil until golden brown.

7. Remove from the oven and cool for a while. Chop into wedges and serve either warm or cooled to room temperature.

Red and White Salad

Serves: 6-8

Ingredients:

- 2/3 cup extra virgin olive oil
- 2 cans (15 ounces each) cannellini beans, drained, rinsed
- 2 heads radicchio, sliced
- 4 tablespoons fresh lemon juice
- 6 large scallions, sliced
- 1 ½ cups Asiago cheese, shaved
- Salt to taste
- Pepper to taste

Method:

1. Whisk together oil and lemon juice in a large bowl.
2. Add rest of the ingredients except cheese and toss well.
3. Add cheese and fold gently.

Roasted Ratatouille with Spaghetti

Serves: 12

Ingredients:

- 4 pints cherry tomatoes or grape tomatoes
- 2 medium yellow squash, chopped
- 10-12 cloves garlic, minced
- 2 medium eggplants, chopped
- 2 medium bell peppers of any color, chopped
- 2 medium zucchini, chopped
- 1 large onion, chopped
- 1 pound whole grain spaghetti, cook according to instructions on the package, retain about 2 cups of the cooked water
- 2 teaspoons fresh thyme (optional)
- 2/3 cup olive oil, divided
- ½ cup cheese, grated
- ¼ cup balsamic vinegar
- Freshly ground black pepper to taste
- 1 teaspoon salt or to taste
- ½ teaspoon red pepper flakes or to taste
- 2 teaspoons dried oregano or 2 tablespoons fresh oregano
- 4 tablespoons fresh basil, chopped
- Parmesan cheese to serve, shredded

Method:

1. Place 2 racks in the oven, one at the top and one at the bottom.
2. Add the cherry tomatoes into a baking dish. Add 4 tablespoons olive oil, salt and pepper. Mix well.

3. Add 4 remaining olive oil, balsamic vinegar, garlic, salt, pepper powder and red pepper flakes into a bowl. Whisk well.
4. Add eggplants, zucchinis, yellow squash, bell pepper and onion into a large bowl. Toss well. Pour the olive oil - vinegar mixture over it. Toss well.
5. Spread the vegetables on to a rimmed baking sheet.
6. Place the baking sheet on the upper rack of the oven. Place the baking dish on the bottom rack of the oven.
7. Bake in a preheated oven at 375 ° F for about 20 minutes.
8. Place the cooked spaghetti in a large bowl.
9. Remove the vegetables and tomatoes from the oven. Turn the vegetables around. If the tomatoes are cooked, they will burst open slightly and will be juicy if not place it back in the oven and roast for a little more time.
10. Add the tomatoes to the bowl of spaghetti.
11. Place the baking sheet with vegetables back into the oven. Bake for further 10 -15 minutes until they are cooked.
12. Transfer into the bowl of spaghetti.
13. Add the retained water and mix well. Sprinkle cheese, oregano, thyme, basil, salt, pepper and red pepper flakes.
14. Toss well and serve with Parmesan cheese.

Penne with Vodka Sauce

Serves: 8

Ingredients:

- 24 ounces whole wheat penne, cook according to the instructions on the package, retain 1 cup of cooked water
- 2 tablespoons unsalted butter
- 2 cloves garlic, minced
- 1 cup vodka
- 1 cup parmesan cheese, grated + extra for garnishing
- Salt to taste
- 2 cans (28 ounces each) whole plum tomatoes
- 4 shallots, minced
- ½ teaspoon red pepper flakes
- 1 1/3 cups heavy cream
- 1 cup fresh basil leaves, torn + extra for garnishing

Method:

1. Add tomatoes into a bowl and crush using your hands.
2. Place a large skillet over medium heat. Add butter. When butter melts, add shallots and sauté until soft.
3. Stir in garlic and red pepper flakes and sauté for a few seconds until fragrant. Turn off the heat.
4. Add tomatoes, vodka and salt and mix well.
5. Place the skillet over medium heat. Stir often and cook for 8-9 minutes.
6. Add heavy cream and cook until slightly thick. Add Parmesan and basil and mix well.

7. Add pasta and toss well. Also, add the retained cooked water and mix well. Add salt and stir.
8. Garnish with Parmesan and basil and serve.

Stuffed Pasta Shells

Serves: 2

Ingredients:

- 1 clove garlic, minced (optional)
- Salt to taste
- Pepper powder to taste
- ¼ teaspoon red chili flakes
- 2/3 cup tofu, crumbled
- ½ teaspoon dried oregano (oregano)
- ¼ cup dairy-free mozzarella cheese, shreds
- 8 jumbo shells
- ¾ cup marinara sauce
- 2 teaspoons vegan basil pesto
- ¼ large eggplant, cut into rounds of ¼ inch thickness
- 1 teaspoon olive oil

Method:

1. Season the eggplant rounds with salt. Place a colander over a bowl and the eggplant rounds in the colander. Let it drain moisture from the eggplant for 10-12 minutes.
2. Place in a preheated oven and broil until soft and light brown. Flip sides a couple of times while it is broiling. Remove from the oven and set aside.
3. Add tofu, oregano, chili flakes and salt into the food processor bowl and pulse until the tofu is broken down into smaller pieces. Add dairy free cheese and pulse until just mixed. Do not over mix. Add eggplant and stir.

4. Taste a bit and adjust the seasonings and pesto if necessary.
5. Meanwhile, cook the pasta shells according to instructions on the package. Cool slightly.
6. Pour ¼ cup marinara sauce on the bottom of a baking dish. Spread it evenly.
7. Stuff each of the shells with the eggplant filling. Place the stuffed shells in the baking dish.
8. Pour marinara sauce over the stuffed shells. Sprinkle olive oil over it.
9. Bake in a preheated oven at 375 ° F for about 20-30 minutes or until heated thoroughly.
10. Serve hot.
11. Serving options: Caesar salad, garlic bread, etc.

Fresh Pasta with Clams and Hot Italian Sausage

Serves: 4

Ingredients:

For dough:

- 1 cup + 2 tablespoons all-purpose flour + extra for dusting
- ½ teaspoon olive oil
- ½ cup semolina flour + extra for dusting
- ½ cup warm water

For assembling:

- 4 tablespoons olive oil
- 4 cloves garlic, peeled, thinly sliced
- ½ cup dry white wine
- 2 tablespoons unsalted butter
- 8 ounces hot Italian sausage, discard casing
- 2 pounds Manila or littleneck clams, scrubbed
- Kosher salt to taste
- 2 tablespoons finely chopped parsley

Method:

1. To make dough: Add all-purpose flour and semolina flour into a large bowl and stir.
2. Pour oil and water and mix until a dough is formed that will be slightly stiff.
3. Dust your countertop with all-purpose flour and place the dough on it. Knead for 8-10 minutes until the dough becomes smooth and bouncy. Wrap the dough in cling wrap and place on the countertop for an hour.

4. Place dough on your countertop and shape the dough into a long log of about 9 inches long and ¾ inch thick. Cut into ½ inch pieces diagonally. Dust the pieces with flour.

5. Take a piece of dough and place it in between your palms. Roll with your palms until 3 inches long. It should be tapering at both the ends. Sprinkle some semolina flour on the pasta and place on a baking sheet that is lined with parchment paper.

6. Repeat the above step with the remaining pieces. Cover the baking sheet with a clean kitchen towel.

7. For assembling: Place a large skillet over medium high heat. Add oil. When the oil is heated, add sausage and sauté until brown. Break it simultaneously as it cooks.

8. Stir in the garlic and cook until aromatic. Stir in the wine and clams. Cover with a lid.

9. Shake the skillet a couple of times. Do not open for about 4-5 minutes. The clams would have opened. Discard the clams that have not opened.

10. Meanwhile, place a pot of water over medium heat. Add a little salt. When the water begins to boil, add pasta and cook for about 3 minutes or until done. Retain about 1-2 cups of the cooked water and discard the rest.

11. Add parsley, butter, pasta and about a cup of the cooked water into the skillet of clams. Toss and cook for 3-5 minutes. Add more of the cooked water if is dry.

12. Add salt and stir.

13. Serve hot.

Pasta all'Amatriciana

Serves: 4

Ingredients:

- 1 can (28 ounces) whole tomatoes, with its juices
- 2 ounces salt cured pork jowl (guanciale), coarsely chopped
- 2 tablespoons olive oil
- 2 tablespoons tomato paste
- ½ teaspoon sugar (optional)
- ½ pound penne pasta or any other tube shaped pasta
- 1 small onion, finely chopped
- 2 ounces pancetta, finely cut
- ½ teaspoon crushed red pepper flakes
- ½ cup dry white wine
- Kosher salt to taste
- Freshly ground pepper to taste
- ¼ cup water
- Pecorino or parmesan cheese, finely grated, to top

Method:

1. Add tomatoes into a blender and blend until smooth.
2. Place a heavy pot over medium heat. Add onion, pancetta, red pepper flakes, guanciale, oil and water. Cook until dry and the fat begins to show.
3. Stir in the tomato paste and cook for a couple of minutes.
4. Stir in the wine and simmer until it is reduced to half its original quantity.

5. Add the blended tomatoes and stir. When it begins to boil, lower the heat and cover partially. Simmer until meat is soft. It should take 25-30 minutes.
6. Add sugar, salt and pepper and stir.
7. Cook pasta following the directions on the package. Drain and add into the sauce. Toss until well combined.
8. Sprinkle pecorino on top and serve.

Vegetable Lasagna

Serves: 4

Ingredients:

- 13-15 ounces Italian tomato sauce (marinara sauce)
- 5 thick lasagna noodles, broken
- ½ cup mushrooms, finely chopped
- ½ cup zucchini, finely chopped
- 2 cloves garlic, finely chopped
- 1 onion, finely chopped
- 1 small egg
- 7.5 ounces part skim ricotta cheese
- ½ cup mozzarella cheese, shredded
- 1 teaspoon dried basil or oregano
- 2 tablespoons fresh parsley

Method:

1. Grease a baking dish with cooking spray.
2. Mix together in a microwave safe bowl, mushroom, onion, garlic and zucchini.
3. Microwave on High for 2-4 minutes. Remove the vegetables and cool for a while. Squeeze excess moisture from the vegetables
4. Add ricotta, egg and basil in a bowl. Mix well.
5. Spread about 1/3 cup of tomato sauce at the bottom of the baking dish
6. Lay about 1/3 of the lasagna pieces over it.
7. Make layers by spreading about 1/3 of each of the following; Vegetables, sauce, ricotta cheese mixture, mozzarella cheese and lasagna.
8. Repeat the above step twice.

9. Finally spread a thin layer of sauce.
10. Bake in a preheated oven at 375 ° F for about 30-40 minutes.
11. Sprinkle parsley over it. Slice and serve.

Chicken Parmesan Lasagna

Serves: 5

Ingredients:

- 25 ounces marinara sauce
- 8 ounces low fat ricotta cheese
- 1 ½ cups chicken, boneless, skinless, cooked, chopped
- 4 ounces no boil lasagna noodles
- 1 ¼ cups part skim mozzarella cheese, shredded, divided

Method:

1. Spread about ½ cup marinara sauce on the bottom of a baking dish. Spread a single layer of lasagna noodles.
2. Place a layer of ricotta cheese followed by ½ cup mozzarella cheese.
3. Layer with half the chicken and ½ cup marinara sauce.
4. Spread another layer of lasagna noodles followed by the remaining chicken and ½ cup mozzarella cheese.
5. Spread the remaining noodles if any and the sauce.
6. Bake in a preheated oven at 375 ° F for about 30-40 minutes.
7. Sprinkle remaining cheese on it during the last 10 minutes of baking. Broil for a couple of minutes if you like a brown top.

Turkey Zucchini Pizza Lasagna

Serves: 4

Ingredients:

For the zoodles:

- ¾ tablespoon salt
- 2 medium zucchinis

For the lasagna:
- ½ pound ground 99% fat-free turkey
- 1 tablespoon olive oil
- Pepper powder to taste
- ½ jar (from a 14 ounce jar) pizza sauce
- 1 tablespoon parmesan cheese, grated
- 4 ounces light mozzarella cheese, grated
- 24 turkey pepperoni slices
- 2 tablespoons slivered olives
- ½ cup onions, chopped
- ½ teaspoon salt
- ¾ tablespoon garlic, peeled, sliced
- 7.5 ounces fat free ricotta cheese
- 1 small egg
- 1 small green pepper, chopped

Method:

1. To make zoodles (zucchini noodles): Make noodles of the zucchini by fixing a julienne blade to the mandolin slicer. Make 1/8-inch slices of the zucchini. Now cut each of the slices lengthwise into 1/8-inch thick strips.

2. Spread the zoodles over a cookie sheet. Sprinkle salt over the zoodles.
3. Bake in a preheated oven at 350 ° F for 10-15 minutes or until light brown. Remove from oven and let it cool.
4. To make lasagna: Place a large pan over medium high heat. Add oil.
5. When the oil is heated, add turkey, onion, garlic, salt to taste and pepper powder. Sauté until the turkey is brown
6. Meanwhile, beat the egg in a bowl. Add ricotta cheese and a pinch of pepper. Beat until well combined.
7. Grease a baking dish with cooking spray.
8. Spread half the pizza sauce all over the bottom of the baking dish.
9. Spread half the turkey evenly over the sauce.
10. Layer with half the zoodles followed by half the ricotta cheese mixture.
11. Spread half the pepperoni slices over the ricotta cheese layer followed by half the mozzarella cheese.
12. Repeat the steps 8-11.
13. Sprinkle the chopped green pepper and olives.
14. Finally top with Parmesan cheese.
15. Cover the dish with aluminum foil. Place the dish in a preheated oven at 375 ° F and bake for about 45 minutes.
16. Remove the foil and bake for 10 minutes. Broil for 2-3 minutes until brown on top.

Chicken Parmigiana

Serves: 2

Ingredients:

- 2 chicken breasts, skinless, boneless, pounded with a meat mallet until thin
- 1 cup all-purpose flour, add a little salt and pepper into it
- 1 cup panko bread crumbs
- Tomato sauce, as required
- 2 tablespoons freshly grated parmesan cheese
- Salt to taste
- Freshly ground black pepper to taste
- 2 large eggs, beaten with a tablespoon of water, salt and pepper
- ½ cup vegetable oil or pure olive oil
- ½ pound fresh mozzarella cheese, thinly sliced
- Basil or parsley leaves to garnish

For tomato sauce:

- 1 tablespoon olive oil
- 2 cloves garlic, smashed with a little salt into a paste
- 8 ounces canned crushed tomatoes
- 1 bay leaf
- ½ Cubano chili pepper, chopped
- 1 medium onion, finely chopped
- 1 can (28 ounces) plum tomatoes with its juices, pureed
- ½ small can tomato paste
- ½ small bunch Italian parsley
- Salt to taste

- Pepper to taste

Method:

1. To make tomato sauce: Place a skillet over medium heat. Add oil. When the oil is heated, add onion and garlic and sauté until translucent.
2. Add rest of the ingredients and stir.
3. Lower the heat and simmer for 15-20 minutes until thick. Turn off the heat. Discard bay leaf.
4. For chicken: Sprinkle salt and pepper over the chicken.
5. Place flour on a plate and dredge chicken in it. Shake to drop off excess flour.
6. Next dip in egg. Shake to drop off excess egg.
7. Place breadcrumbs on a plate. Finally, dredge chicken in breadcrumbs.
8. Place a pan over medium heat. Add oil. When the oil is heated, place chicken in it and cook until golden brown on both the sides.
9. Remove with a slotted spoon and place on a baking sheet. Spread tomato sauce over it.
10. Place mozzarella slices over it. Sprinkle salt and pepper and place Parmesan cheese on top.
11. Bake in a preheated oven at 400 ° F for about 7-8 minutes or until it is cooked and cheese melts.
12. Sprinkle basil and serve.

Chicken with Sage

Serves: 2

Ingredients:

- 1 ½ tablespoons butter
- 2 chicken breasts, skinless, boneless, pounded until thin
- 1 tablespoon lemon juice
- ¼ teaspoon cornstarch
- 6 sage leaves
- ½ cup chicken broth
- 1 tablespoon capers

Method:

1. Place a skillet over medium heat. Add butter. When butter melts, place chicken and cook for 6 minutes. Flip sides and cook the other side for 6 minutes.
2. Remove with a slotted spoon and place on a plate lined with paper towels. Set aside.
3. Add rest of the ingredients into a skillet and whisk well.
4. Place skillet over medium low heat. Simmer for4-5 minutes.
5. Divide chicken into serving plates. Pour gravy on top and serve.

Italian Red Pepper Chicken

Serves: 3

Ingredients:

- 1 pound chicken breast, skinless, boneless, chopped
- 2 medium red peppers, sliced
- 1 large clove garlic, minced
- 1 medium onion, sliced
- 10 ounces canned, diced, fire roasted tomatoes
- 1 tablespoon balsamic vinegar
- ½ teaspoon red pepper flakes or to taste
- ½ teaspoon salt
- ½ teaspoon pepper
- 2 teaspoons Italian seasoning

Method:

1. Add all the ingredients into a Dutch oven. Mix well.
2. Cover and cook until chicken is tender.
3. Serve hot.

Chicken and Artichoke Panini

Serves: 2

Ingredients:

- 4 slices bread
- 1 cooked chicken breast, skinless, boneless, sliced
- A handful fresh parsley, chopped
- ¼ cup cream cheese spread
- ¼ cup marinated artichoke hearts, drained, quartered
- Salt to taste
- Pepper to taste

Method:

1. Apply 1-tablespoon cream cheese on each slice of bread.
2. Divide and place chicken, artichoke and parsley on 2 slices of bread. Sprinkle salt and pepper.
3. Cover with the remaining 2 bread slices, cheese side facing down.
4. Place in a preheated Panini press and cook until the way you like it grilled.

Pulled Pork Ragu

Serves: 5

Ingredients:

- 9 ounces pork tenderloin
- 3 cloves garlic, peeled, smashed
- 3.5 ounces jarred roasted red peppers
- 1 large red onion, chopped
- 1 can (14.5 ounces) crushed tomatoes
- 1 tablespoon fresh oregano, chopped
- 1 sprig fresh thyme
- 2 teaspoons fresh parsley, chopped, divided
- 1 bay leaf
- Pepper to taste
- ½ teaspoon kosher salt
- 1 teaspoon oil

Method:

1. Place a Dutch oven over medium heat. Add oil and heat.
2. Sprinkle salt and pepper over the pork and cook until light brown.
3. Add rest of the ingredients except 1-teaspoon parsley and stir.
4. Add a little water and stir.
5. Lower the heat. Cover and cook until meat is tender.
6. Remove the meat with a slotted spoon and place on your cutting board.
7. When cool enough to handle, shred with a pair of forks.

8. Add it back into the pot. Heat thoroughly. Transfer into a bowl. Garnish with parsley.
9. Serve over your favorite pasta.

Spicy Italian Pork Meatballs

Serves: 8

Ingredients:

For meatballs:

- 2 pounds ground pork
- 1 cup panko bread crumbs Italian style
- A handful fresh basil, chopped
- 2 teaspoons dried Italian herb seasoning
- 1 teaspoon crushed red pepper flakes
- 2 eggs
- ½ cup parmesan cheese, shredded
- 4 teaspoons garlic, finely chopped
- 1 teaspoon salt

For marinara sauce:

- 2 tablespoons olive oil
- ½ teaspoon crushed red pepper flakes
- ½ teaspoon salt
- 6 cloves garlic, crushed
- 2 cans (14.5 ounces each) fire roasted tomatoes, crushed, with its liquid
- 16 medium basil leaves

Method:

1. To make meatballs: Add all the ingredients of meatballs into a bowl and mix well.
2. Scoop out 1 tablespoon of the mixture and make a ball. Repeat this to make the remaining balls.

3. Place the balls on a rimmed baking sheet.
4. Bake in a preheated oven at 400 ° F for about 15-18 minutes or until it is cooked through.
5. Meanwhile, make the sauce as follows: Place a saucepan over medium heat. Add oil. When the oil is heated, add garlic and red pepper flakes and sauté until aromatic.
6. Stir in the tomatoes, salt and basil. Mix well.
7. Lower heat and simmer until slightly thick. Turn off the heat. Cool for a few minutes.
8. Transfer into a blender. Blend until smooth.
9. Pour over the meatballs and serve with your favorite pasta.

Spicy Italian Pork Cutlets

Serves: 2

Ingredients:

- 2 tablespoons extra-virgin olive oil, divided
- Salt to taste
- Pepper powder to taste
- 1 medium tomato, chopped
- 2 tablespoons dry white wine
- Red pepper flakes to taste
- 2 boneless pork chops, pounded to ¼ inch thickness
- 2 cloves garlic, thinly sliced
- 3 tablespoons chicken broth
- A handful fresh parsley, minced

Method:

1. Place a skillet over medium high heat. Add 1-tablespoon oil and let the oil heat.
2. Sprinkle salt and pepper over the pork chops and place in the skillet. Cook until brown on both the sides. Remove pork with a slotted spoon and set aside on a plate.
3. Add 1-tablespoon oil into the same skillet. When the oil is heated, add garlic and sauté until fragrant.
4. Add tomato, wine, red pepper flakes, chicken broth and parsley. Mix well. Cook for a couple of minutes.
5. Add the pork back into the skillet and cook until the pork has an internal temperature of 145 ° F.
6. Serve pork with sauce.

Beef and Mortadella Meatballs in Tomato Sauce

Serves: 8

Ingredients:

- ½ cup olive oil
- 2 medium carrots, finely chopped
- 1 cup tomato paste
- 2 cups heavy cream
- Freshly ground pepper to taste
- 1 pound mortadella, cut into ¼ inch pieces
- 1 pound ground beef, preferably chuck
- 4 large eggs
- ½ cup fresh parsley, chopped
- Grana Padano cheese, to serving
- 2 medium onions, finely chopped
- 2 stalks celery, finely chopped
- 14 ounces canned crushed tomatoes
- 2 teaspoons kosher salt + extra
- 2/3 cup fine fresh breadcrumbs
- ¼ cup fresh oregano, chopped

Method:

1. Place a large heavy pot over medium high heat. Add oil. When the oil is heated, add onion, celery, carrot, salt and pepper. Sauté until onions are translucent.
2. Stir in the tomato paste and sauté for 4-5 minutes.
3. Add tomatoes, salt, pepper and cream and stir. When it begins to boil, lower the heat and let it simmer.
4. Meanwhile to make meatballs, add mortadella, beef, breadcrumbs, eggs, parsley, salt and oregano into a bowl and mix until well incorporated.

5. Make small balls of the mixture (about 1 ½ inches diameter) and place on a plate.
6. Drop the meatballs in the simmering sauce. Cover with lid. Simmer until meatballs are cooked. It may take 40-50 minutes.
7. Garnish with Grana Padano and serve.

Italian Casserole

Serves: 10-12

Ingredients:

- 1 pound Italian sausage
- 2 pounds ground beef
- ¼ cup onions, chopped
- 2 cans (8 ounce each) tomato sauce
- Pepper powder to taste
- 3 cloves garlic, minced
- 1 pound fresh mushrooms, sliced
- Salt to taste
- Italian seasoning to taste
- 1 cup mozzarella cheese, shredded

For the topping:

- 1 cup sour cream
- 1 teaspoon garlic powder
- 1 cup parmesan, shredded
- 1 cup mayonnaise
- 1 teaspoon pepper powder
- 2 cups mozzarella cheese

Method:

1. Place a nonstick skillet over medium heat. Add the beef, sausages, onions, and mushrooms. Sauté until the beef is browned.
2. Add salt and pepper. Mix well. Remove the excess fat. Add garlic, tomato sauce, and Italian seasoning. Add more salt, pepper, and Italian seasoning if necessary.

3. Transfer the contents into a greased baking dish.
4. Mix together all the ingredients of the topping. Spread over the meat in the baking dish.
5. Bake in a preheated oven at 350 degree F for 40 minutes or until well browned.

Eggplant Pizza

Serves: 2

Ingredients:

- 1 pound ground beef
- 1 big eggplant, cut into ½ inch round slices
- 1 medium onion, chopped
- 4 ounces tomato sauce
- 2 cloves garlic, sliced
- Salt and pepper, to taste
- 2 cups shredded cheese
- 1/4 cup olive oil
- ¼ teaspoon ground cinnamon (optional)
- 1/4 cup fresh oregano, chopped

Method:

1. Brush some olive oil on the eggplant slices and place them on a greased baking sheet.
2. Preheat the oven and bake the eggplants at 400°F for about 20 minutes.
3. Heat a skillet over medium flame and add 1-tablespoon oil to the same. Add the garlic and onion and sauté until onions become translucent.
4. Add the beef and sauté it until it gets brown. Add the tomato sauce, and season with salt and pepper.
5. Stir occasionally and let it cook for another 15 minutes.
6. Spread the beef mixture the baked eggplant slices.
7. Sprinkle with cheese and oregano and toss in the oven for a few minutes, until the cheese melts.
8. Serve hot.

Classic Margherita Pizza

Serves: 3

Ingredients:

- ½ package refrigerated classic crust pizza dough
- ¼ cup canned crushed tomatoes
- ¼ cup small fresh basil leaves
- 2 cloves garlic, sliced
- ½ tablespoon olive oil
- 4 ounces fresh mozzarella cheese pearls, pat dried

Method:

1. Place rack in the oven in the lowest position.
2. Take an ungreased baking sheet and place an oven safe parchment paper on it. Unroll the dough on it. Smear oil all over the dough.
3. Spread tomato over the crust.
4. Sprinkle garlic slices over it. Sprinkle mozzarella cheese.
5. Bake in a preheated oven at 400 ° F for about 7-8 minutes or until it is cooked and cheese melts.
6. Garnish with basil. Cut into 3 equal slices and serve.

Italian Eggplant and Lentils

Serves: 8

Ingredients:

- 4 medium eggplants, halved
- 2 medium brown onions, diced
- 2 cans (14.5 ounces each) lentils, rinsed, drained
- 4 cloves garlic, crushed
- 3 tablespoons fresh basil, chopped
- 2 large zucchinis, grated
- 2 tablespoons olive oil
- 1 ½ cups parmesan cheese, grated
- 4 medium tomatoes
- 1 cup vegetable broth
- ½ tablespoon dried Italian seasoning
- 4 tablespoons tomato paste, unsalted
- ¼ teaspoon red pepper flakes
- Salt to taste
- Pepper to taste

Method:

1. Place a sheet of baking paper over a baking sheet.
2. Take a spoon and scoop out the flesh of the eggplant. Keep the outer covering intact, leaving about 1 cm of the flesh. In other words, you have a boat like an eggplant casing. Set aside the casings.
3. Finely chop the scooped flesh of the eggplant.
4. Place a nonstick skillet over medium heat. Add oil. When the oil is heated, add onion and garlic and sauté for a couple of minutes.

5. Add eggplant and cook until soft. Add zucchini, tomatoes, tomato paste, salt, seasoning and spices. Mix well.
6. Add lentils and mix well. Cook for a few minutes until thick.
7. Place eggplant cases on the prepared baking sheet.
8. Divide the eggplant mixture among the eggplant cases. Sprinkle cheese on top.
9. Bake in a preheated oven at 400 ° F for about 20 minutes.

Italian White Beans

Serves: 3

Ingredients:

- 16-18 ounces canned diced tomatoes with Italian seasoning
- 4 cloves garlic, sliced
- 2 cans (14.5 ounces each) white beans, Great Northern or Navy beans
- 3 tablespoons fresh parsley, chopped
- Pepper to taste
- Salt to taste
- 2 cups hot vegetable broth
- 2 teaspoons Italian seasoning
- 2 teaspoons balsamic vinegar
- 1 bay leaf
- Crushed red pepper flakes to taste

Method:

1. Add all the ingredients into a skillet. Mix well. Place the skillet over medium heat.
2. Simmer for 20-30 minutes. Discard the bay leaf.
3. Serve hot.

Butternut Squash Risotto

Serves: 8

Ingredients:

- 2 cups Arborio rice or medium grained rice
- 2 butternut squashes, peeled, deseeded, cut into 1/2 inch cubes
- 4 teaspoons olive oil or butter
- 1 onion, chopped
- 1 cup white wine
- 9-10 cups hot vegetable stock
- Salt to taste
- Pepper powder to taste
- 2 tablespoons fresh sage or 2 teaspoons dried sage
- 2-3 tablespoons parmesan cheese

Method:

1. Place a large saucepan over medium high heat. Add oil. When oil is heated, add onion, butternut squash, a little salt and pepper.
2. Sauté until the squash becomes soft.
3. Lower the heat to medium and add rice. Stir-fry for a few minutes until the rice turns opaque.
4. Add wine and cook until wine has almost evaporated.
5. Add stock (½ cup) a little at a time and continue cooking until stock evaporates each time.
6. Keep repeating step 5 until rice is cooked. Add more stock if you find the rice is not cooked well.
7. Add cheese and sage and mix well.
8. Remove from heat and serve hot.

Spring Green Risotto

Serves: 4

Ingredients:

- 2 packages (9 ounces each) frozen chopped spinach, thaw slightly
- 2 leeks, finely chopped
- 2 cups packed fresh kale, chopped, discard hard stems and ribs
- 2 cups short grain Arborio rice, rinsed
- 2 cups dry white wine
- ½ cup olive oil
- 4 cloves garlic, minced
- Salt to taste
- Freshly ground pepper to taste
- 8 cups chicken broth
- Grated parmesan cheese (optional)

Method:

1. Place a large saucepan over medium low heat. Add oil. When oil is heated, add leek and garlic
2. Sauté until the leek becomes soft.
3. Add kale, salt and pepper and cook until kale wilts.
4. Add rice. Stir-fry for a few minutes until the rice turns opaque.
5. Add wine and cook until wine has almost evaporated.
6. Add stock (½ cup) a little at a time and continue cooking until stock evaporates each time.
7. Keep repeating step 6 until rice is cooked. Add more stock if you find the rice is not cooked well.
8. Add spinach and mix well. Add cheese and mix well.
9. Remove from heat and serve hot.

Tomato Risotto

Serves: 3

Ingredients:

- ½ small onion, chopped
- ¼ cup dry white wine
- ½ tablespoon unsalted butter
- 3 oil poached tomato halves, coarsely chopped
- 1 tablespoon olive oil
- ¾ cup Arborio rice
- ½ cup tomato water
- 1 tablespoon parmesan cheese, grated + extra to serve
- Kosher salt to taste
- Freshly ground black pepper to taste
- Water, as required

Method:

1. Place a large saucepan over medium heat. Add oil. When the oil is heated, add onion and sauté until translucent.
2. Stir in the rice and sauté until opaque. Add wine and stir constantly until it is dry.
3. Add water, ¼ cup at a time and cook each time until dry. Cook until rice is tender but not overcooked.
4. Add tomato water, Parmesan cheese, butter, salt and pepper. Stir frequently until almost dry.
5. Add oil-poached tomatoes and mix well.
6. Garnish with Parmesan cheese and serve.

Fritto Misto

Serves:

Ingredients:

- 8 ounces large shrimp, halved lengthwise (make sure they are peeled and deveined)
- 8 ounces squid or baby octopus tentacles
- 2 cups all-purpose flour
- 2 teaspoons baking powder
- 2 cups cornstarch
- 1 teaspoon kosher salt + extra
- 2 leeks, halved lengthwise, separate the layers
- ½ small squash, scrubbed, and thinly cut
- 2 lemons, very thinly sliced into rounds, deseeded
- Lemon wedges to serve
- ½ cup fresh sage leaves
- 1 cup fresh parsley leaves, chopped
- 4 cups chilled club soda
- ¼ small fennel bulb, very thinly sliced lengthwise
- 4 ounces shiitake or maitake mushrooms, trimmed, torn into bite size pieces
- Vegetable oil, to deep fry, as required

Method:

1. Place a small deep pan over medium heat. Add oil up to half. Let the oil heat.
2. Add flour, baking powder, cornstarch and salt into a bowl and stir. Pour club soda and stir until well combined. Do not over mix. Add some of each of the following in the batter – lemon slices, shrimp, squid,

lemon slices, leeks, squash, fennel bulb and mushrooms, sage, parsley.

3. When the oil is heated to 375° F, lift the ingredients from the batter and add into the hot oil. Fry until crisp. Separate the ingredients while frying with a slotted spoon.

4. Remove with a slotted spoon and place over plates lined with paper towels. Sprinkle salt over it.

5. Repeat steps 3-4 to fry the remaining ingredients, each time the oil should be heated (step 3).

6. Serve with lemon wedges.

Roasted Vegetables Antipasto Plate

Serves: 2-3

Ingredients:

- ½ tin (from a 2 ounce tin) oil packed anchovies, drained, finely chopped
- 1 pound cauliflower, cut into large florets
- ½ pound medium carrots, scrubbed, cut diagonally into ¾ inch thick pieces
- ½ teaspoon lemon zest, grated
- 3 ½ tablespoons olive oil, divided plus extra for serving
- Kosher salt to taste
- Freshly ground pepper to taste
- ¼ teaspoon dried oregano
- 2 tablespoons panko breadcrumbs

Method:

1. Mash the anchovies with the back of a spoon until a paste is formed that is smooth in texture.
2. Add 2 tablespoons oil and stir. Add cauliflower, salt and pepper and toss until well combined. Transfer on to a rimmed baking sheet.
3. Add 1-tablespoon oil, carrots, oregano, salt and pepper into a bowl and toss until well combined. Transfer on to another baking sheet.
4. Place the baking sheet with carrots on the upper rack in the oven.
5. Place the baking sheet with cauliflowers on the bottom rack.

6. Bake in a preheated oven at 425 ° F for about 15-20 minutes.
7. Turn the carrots and cauliflower halfway through baking.
8. Remove the carrots from the oven and shift the cauliflower to the upper rack. Let it bake for 15-20 minutes or until tender. Turn the cauliflower a couple of times while it is baking.
9. Sprinkle lemon zest over the carrots. Set aside.
10. Place a small skillet over medium heat. Add ½ tablespoon oil. When the oil is heated, add panko breadcrumbs and sauté until golden brown in color. Stir frequently.
11. Sprinkle salt over it. Remove with a slotted spoon and place on a plate lined with paper towels.
12. Trickle oil over the carrots. Sprinkle panko crumbs over the cauliflower and serve.

Baked Parmesan Tomatoes

Serves: 8

Ingredients:

- 8 tomatoes, halved horizontally
- 2 teaspoons fresh oregano, minced
- 8 teaspoons extra-virgin olive oil
- ½ cup parmesan cheese, freshly grated
- ½ teaspoon salt
- Freshly ground pepper to taste

Method:

1. Lay the tomatoes in the baking sheet, with the cut side facing up. Sprinkle Parmesan, salt, pepper and oregano.
2. Trickle some oil over it.
3. Bake in a preheated oven at 450 ° F for about 15-20 minutes.
4. Serve.

Chapter Four: Italian Dessert Recipes

Balsamic Berries

Serves: 8

Ingredients:

- 1 1/3 cups white balsamic vinegar
- 1 cup heavy cream, chilled
- 6 cups strawberries, sliced
- Pepper to taste
- ½ cup sugar
- 1 cup mascarpone cheese, chilled
- 1 teaspoon lemon zest

Method:

1. Pour vinegar into a small saucepan. Add 4 tablespoons sugar.
2. Place over medium heat. Simmer until it is reduced to half its original quantity. Turn off the heat.
3. Add cream, remaining sugar and mascarpone into a mixing bowl. Beat with an electric mixer until fluffy. Do not beat for too long.
4. Divide berries into serving bowls. Drizzle syrup on top.
5. Sprinkle lemon zest. Spoon whipped cream top. Sprinkle pepper on top and serve.

Italian Castagnaccio (Chestnut Cake)

Serves: 12-16

Ingredients:

- 3 cups chestnut flour
- 3 cups water
- 2 tablespoons coconut sugar or fine caster sugar
- 4 tablespoons extra virgin olive oil
- ½ cup raisins or chocolate chips
- 1/4 cup pine nuts
- ½ cup walnuts or toasted, peeled hazelnuts
- 1/8 teaspoon salt
- 2 large sprigs of rosemary use leaves only.
- Maple syrup or agave nectar honey as required to serve

Method:

1. Add chestnut flour, sugar, salt and half the water into a bowl and whisk until well combined.
2. Add a tablespoon of water at a time and whisk until smooth. Remember that the batter should be smooth and dropping consistency but not runny. Stop adding water if you think the consistency is right.
3. Add half the raisins to the batter and fold.
4. Grease 2-3 pie dishes with a little oil and place in a preheated oven for a minute.
5. Remove the pie dishes from the oven. Pour batter into the pie dishes.
6. Drizzle the remaining oil over it and fold lightly.
7. Sprinkle remaining raisins, walnuts, pine nuts and rosemary.

8. Bake in a preheated oven at 400 ° F for about 20 - 25 minutes or until the top is cracked and brown.
9. Remove from oven and cool. Slice and serve either warm or cold with honey.

Tiramisu

Serves: 4

Ingredients:

- 3 large egg yolks
- 6 tablespoons whole milk
- ¾ cup espresso or strong coffee, at room temperature
- 6 tablespoons sugar
- 2 containers (8 ounces each) mascarpone cheese, at room temperature
- ¼ cup brandy or cognac
- 2 tablespoons cocoa powder
- 15-16 crisp Italian ladyfingers (savoiardi)
- Bittersweet chocolate, shaved, as required

Method:

1. Place a large sheet of plastic wrap in a square 4-5 inch baking dish. Let it hang from all the sides. Set aside.
2. Add iced water into a large bowl and set aside.
3. To make custard: Add yolks and sugar into a heatproof bowl. Place the bowl in a double boiler. Stir frequently until sugar is dissolved.
4. Add milk and whisk constantly until creamy and light. A cooking thermometer when inserted should show 170 ° F.
5. Remove the bowl from the double boiler and place in the bowl of chilled water.
6. Whisk constantly until the custard cools.
7. Place mascarpone cheese into a bowl. Pour custard into it and fold until well combined and smooth. Do not over mix.

8. Add espresso and brandy into a shallow bowl and mix well.
9. Dip one lady finger at a time in the espresso mixture for a few seconds and place in the baking dish. Repeat the above step with the remaining ladyfingers. Make 2 rows of 1/3 the biscuits.
10. Spread 1/3 the custard over it.
11. Repeat steps 9 and 10 twice more, place biscuits in opposite direction in each layer.
12. Sprinkle cocoa powder. Cover the dish with the plastic that is hanging on the sides.
13. Chill for 4-8 hours.
14. Invert the tiramisu onto a plate. Invert again from the plate to another plate.
15. Unwrap. Shave chocolate directly on the tiramisu and serve.

Italian Cream Cheese and Ricotta Cheesecake

Serves: 4

Ingredients:

- 8 ounces cream cheese, softened
- ¾ cup white sugar
- ½ tablespoon lemon juice
- 1 ½ tablespoons cornstarch
- ¼ cup butter, melted, cooled
- 8 ounces ricotta cheese
- 2 eggs
- ½ teaspoon vanilla extract
- 1 ½ tablespoons flour
- ½ pint sour cream

Method:

1. Grease a small (6 inch) springform pan with a little butter. Set aside.
2. Add cream cheese and ricotta cheese into a bowl and stir well.
3. Add sugar and beat until creamy.
4. Add eggs, vanilla extract, lemon juice, flour, cornstarch and butter into the bowl; add one ingredient at a time. Beat well each time.
5. Add sour cream and mix well.
6. Pour into the prepared pan.
7. Bake in a preheated oven at 350° F until the center is set. It may take an hour.

Homemade Italian Cream Sodas

Serves: 2

Ingredients:

- 1 cup club soda
- 2 tablespoons half and half
- Whipped cream to top
- 6 tablespoons Torani syrup
- Ice cubes, as required
- 2 cherries to garnish

Method:

1. Take 2 glasses and add ice cubes in it.
2. Add ½ cup club soda into each glass.
3. Divide the Torani syrup among the glasses.
4. Add 1 tablespoon half and half into each glass.

Hazelnut Gelato

Serves: 6

Ingredients:

- 6 cups whole milk
- 10 egg yolks
- 2 cups heavy cream
- 1 1/3 cups sugar
- 1 pound hazelnuts, roasted, discard skin, coarsely ground

Method:

1. Add milk and cream into a saucepan. Place the saucepan over medium heat. Heat until warm. Turn off the heat.
2. Add whole milk and hazelnuts into a large saucepan. Place the saucepan over medium heat.
3. When it begins to boil, turn off the heat and cover with a lid. Set aside for an hour.
4. Pass the mixture through a strainer, placed over a bowl. Press the nuts to remove as much milk as possible. Set aside the milk and discard the nuts.
5. Add yolks and sugar into a bowl and whisk with an electric mixer until pale yellow in color.
6. Add about 2 tablespoons of warm milk mixture into the yolk whisking simultaneously. Repeat with the remaining mixture until all of it is added.
7. Pour the egg mixture back into the saucepan.
8. Place the saucepan over low heat. Stir constantly with a heatproof spatula and cook until thick. It should coat the back of the spoon. Remove from heat and

transfer into a bowl. If you find the egg is curdling, turn off heat immediately.

9. Add cream and stir.
10. Pass the mixture through a strainer placed over a bowl. Place the bowl in an ice bath. Cover with plastic and refrigerate for a few hours.
11. Pour into an ice cream maker and churn the ice cream following the manufacturer's instructions.
12. Transfer into a freezer safe container. Freeze until it sets according to the way you like it.
13. Alternately, pour the mixture into a freezer safe container and freeze. After about an hour of freezing, remove the ice cream from the freezer and whisk well. Place it back in the freezer.
14. Beat again after 30-40 minutes.
15. Repeat the above step a couple of times more until well frozen without ice crystals.

Pink Grapefruit Blueberry Sorbet

Serves: 2

Ingredients:

- 2 cups pink grapefruit juice
- 1 cup white sugar or to taste, powdered
- 2 cups fresh or frozen blueberries
- ¼ cup vodka (optional)

Method:

1. Add all the ingredients into a blender and blend until well combined.
2. Pour into an ice cream maker and churn following the manufacturer's instructions.
3. Alternately, pour the mixture into a freezer safe container and freeze. After about an hour of freezing, remove the ice cream from the freezer and whisk well. Place it in the freezer and beat again after 30-40 minutes.
4. Scoop into bowls and serve.

Italian Christmas Cookies

Serves: 12

Ingredients:

- 2 eggs
- ¼ cup butter
- 1 ¾ cups flour
- 1 cup confectioners' sugar, sifted
- 3 teaspoons water
- ½ cup sugar
- 1 teaspoon vanilla
- 2 teaspoons baking powder
- Sprinkles if desired

Method:

1. Pass the flour and baking powder through a fine sieve, placed over a bowl.
2. Add butter and sugar into a mixing bowl. Beat with an electric mixer until creamy.
3. Add eggs and vanilla and beat until well combined. Add the flour mixture and stir until dough is formed. Dust your hands with flour and knead the dough. Make 12 equal portions of the dough.
4. Take one piece of dough and place it in between your palms. Roll it between your palms and shape into a log. Spin the log into any shape. Place on a baking sheet that is greased with a little oil.
5. Repeat the above step with the remaining portions.
6. Bake in a preheated oven at 375° F for 10 minutes.
7. Add confectioners' sugar, water and vanilla into a bow and beat until creamy.

8. Line a baking sheet with wax paper. Dredge the cookies in the icing and place on the prepared baking sheet. Sprinkle some sprinkles if desired.

Italian Hazelnut Cookies

Serves: 18-20

Ingredients:

- 1 cup hazelnuts, toasted, skinned
- 2 large egg whites
- ¼ teaspoon vanilla extract
- 10 tablespoons sugar
- ¼ teaspoon salt

Method:

1. Place rack in the central position in the oven. Line baking sheet with a sheet of parchment paper. Set aside.
2. Add hazelnuts and sugar in the food processor and grind to a fine powder. Transfer to a bowl.
3. Add egg whites into a third bowl and beat with an electric mixer. Set the mixer on high speed. Beat until stiff peaks are formed.
4. Gently fold in the egg whites into hazelnut – sugar mixture. Add vanilla extract and mix well.
5. Drop tablespoonful of the batter, all over the baking sheet. Leave 2 inches space between 2 cookies.
6. Bake in a preheated oven at 325° F for 25-30 minutes.
7. Remove from the oven and let it cool completely. Store in an airtight container.

Amaretto Biscotti

Serves: 15

Ingredients:

- 1 cup + 2 tablespoons all-purpose flour + extra for dusting
- ¼ teaspoon ground cinnamon
- 2 ½ tablespoons unsalted butter, at room temperature
- 1 large egg
- ½ teaspoon vanilla extract
- ½ teaspoon almond extract
- ½ cup raw almonds
- 1 ounce white chocolate, chopped
- 1 teaspoon baking powder
- ¼ teaspoon salt
- ½ cup sugar
- 1 tablespoon amaretto liqueur
- ½ cup chocolate covered almonds
- 1 ounce semisweet chocolate, chopped

Method:

1. Place a sheet of parchment paper on a baking sheet.
2. Add flour, cinnamon, baking powder and salt in a bowl and stir.
3. Add butter and sugar into a mixing bowl. Beat with an electric mixer at medium high speed until it turns fluffy and pale in color.
4. Add liqueur, eggs, almond extract and vanilla extract and beat well.

5. Lower the speed to low speed. Add the flour mixture and beat until just combined. Do not overbeat.
6. Add chocolate chips and fold gently.
7. Dredge your hands in flour and shape the dough into a log of about 12 inches long and 3 inches diameter.
8. Place on the prepared baking sheet.
9. Place rack in the center of the oven.
10. Bake in a preheated oven at 350° F for 25 minutes or until the log is puffed up.
11. Remove from the oven and cool for 10 minutes on the baking sheet.
12. Place the log on your cutting board. Cut into 1 inch thick pieces. Place on the baking sheet, with the cut side facing down.
13. Place the baking sheet back in the oven. Lower the temperature to 250° F. Bake for about 45 minutes. Flip sides half way through baking. Remove the baking sheet from the oven and let the cookies cool on the baking sheet.
14. Remove the cookies carefully with a metal spatula and cool on a wire rack.
15. Place white chocolate in a small microwave safe bowl. Place semi-sweet chocolate in another microwave safe bowl. Microwave on High for a minute or so until melted. Stir every 30 seconds.
16. Trickle both the chocolates on the biscotti and cool for a while until the chocolate is set.
17. Serve.

Florentine Cookies

Serves: 35-40

Ingredients:

- 3 ½ cups almonds, blanched, sliced
- Zest of 2 oranges, finely grated
- 1 ½ cups sugar
- 10 tablespoons butter, unsalted
- 2 ounces dark chocolate, chopped (optional) to serve
- 6 tablespoons all-purpose flour
- ½ teaspoon salt
- 4 tablespoons heavy cream
- 4 tablespoons corn syrup
- 1 teaspoon vanilla extract

Method:

1. Line 2 large baking sheets with parchment paper.
2. Add almonds into a blender and blend until finely chopped. Transfer into a bowl. Add salt, orange zest and flour and mix until well combined.
3. Place a saucepan over medium heat. Add sugar, cream, corn syrup and butter and stir frequently until the sugar dissolves completely. Turn off the heat and add vanilla extract. Mix well.
4. Mix together the cream mixture and almonds. Set aside for 30 minutes.
5. Make balls of the mixture and place on the prepared baking sheets. Leave a gap of 3-4 inches between 2 balls.

6. Bake in a preheated oven at 350° F for about 10-11 minutes. Rotate the pan halfway through baking. Bake in batches.
7. When done, remove from the oven and cool on a wire rack.
8. If you are using chocolate, melt the chocolate in a double boiler or a microwave.
9. Drizzle chocolate on all the cookies and serve.
10. To make sandwich cookies: Spoon some chocolate on one cookie. Cover with another cookie.
11. Repeat the above step to make the remaining sandwich.
12. Place the cookies in an airtight container. It can last for 3 days.

Cannoli Parfait

Serves: 2

Ingredients:

- 1 cup ricotta
- 4 tablespoons honey or to taste
- 2 teaspoons vanilla
- Ground cinnamon to sprinkle (optional)
- 1 cup almond cookies, broken into pieces
- Chocolate chips, as required
- 4-5 almonds, slivered, to garnish

Method:

1. Take 2 parfait glasses. Divide the almond cookies among the glasses.
2. Spoon ½ cup ricotta over it. Drizzle vanilla over it. Sprinkle chocolate chips.
3. Trickle some honey on top. Garnish with almond slivers and serve.

Zabaglione with Berries

Serves: 8

Ingredients:

- 2 quart strawberries, sliced
- 2 egg whites
- 10 egg yolks
- ½ cup sugar, divided
- 2 tablespoons marsala wine
- A pinch salt
- 1 teaspoon vanilla extract
- Biscotti to serve

Method:

1. Add strawberries into a bowl. Add 2 tablespoons sugar and stir. Let it sit for 10 minutes.
2. Divide the strawberries into 8 glasses.
3. Add whites, yolks, remaining sugar, vanilla, Marsala wine and salt into a heatproof bowl.
4. Place the bowl in a double boiler. The double boiler should be placed on medium-high heat. Stir vigorously until thick and smooth. Turn off the heat and spoon the warm custard over the berries.
5. Top with biscotti and serve right away.

Mini Zeppoles

Serves: 2

Ingredients:

- ½ pound refrigerated pizza dough
- Vegetable oil, as required
- Confectioners' sugar to sprinkle or dredge

Method:

1. Cut the dough into 1-inch pieces. Roll each piece into a ball.
2. Place a small deep pan over medium heat. Add oil up to half. Let the oil heat.
3. When the oil is heated to 375° F, fry the balls in batches until golden brown on all the sides.
4. Remove with a slotted spoon and place on a plate lined with paper towels.
5. Sprinkle or dredge the balls with confectioners' sugar.
6. Serve.

Conclusion

Here ends our journey to Italy and a quick crash course in Italian cuisine. I hope you found the book informative and interesting.

Italian cuisine is definitely one of the most loved, delicious, rich and healthy cuisines from across the world.

The recipes often call for fresh herbs, vegetables and fruit. However, these can be replaced with frozen and canned foods as well. It is also possible to change and replace certain ingredients if you don't like them or if they are not available. You can take a judgment call on the same and replace certain ingredients to improve the texture or flavor of the dish.

Modify and experiment with these recipes and create your very own personalized Italian recipes. Do not let cooking become a chore. Rather, make it a fun activity. The recipes in this book are simple, easy to make and delicious. All the recipes have been tested and tasted so the end result will leave you satisfied.

Finally, if you enjoyed this book then I'd like to ask you for a favor. Will you be kind enough to leave a review for this book on Amazon? It would be greatly appreciated!

Thank you and good luck!

Irish Cookbook

Traditional Irish Recipes Made Easy

The information herein is offered for informational purposes solely and is universal as so. The presentation of the information is without a contract or any type of guarantee assurance.

The trademarks that are used are without any consent, and the publication of the trademark is without permission or backing by the trademark owner. All trademarks and brands within this book are for clarifying purposes only and are the owned by the owners themselves, not affiliated with this document.

www.grizzlypublishing.com

Table of Contents

Introduction

Thank you for choosing this book, '*Irish Cookbook: Traditional Irish Recipes Made Easy.*'

Most people believe that Irish food comprises only of mutton and potatoes. They do not know how wrong they are. The cooking techniques and food of Ireland were influenced by the rich culture and heritage of the Irish people. Irish food draws its ingredients from the available land, sea, pasturelands and moors in Ireland. Family and home play a rich role in Ireland. If you happened to pass by an Irish family's house, you will find that they all cook together in the kitchen and enjoy a hearty meal at the dining table.

History of Irish food

Irish food has been influenced by many cultures over the centuries, right from the Celts who inhabited Ireland between 600 and 500 BC and the English and the Vikings who settled in Ireland between the 16th and 17th centuries. Before potato was introduced to the Irish in the 16th century, meat was an important ingredient used in their food. This meat was often consumed only by the rich while the poor only consumed milk, cheese, butter and offal, which were complemented with barley and grains to add some nourishment.

Potato – A Blessing and a Curse

Potatoes were introduced in Ireland in the 16th century since Ireland was the perfect place to grow potatoes. The cool and damp climate allowed every family to grow potatoes in their home garden. This vegetable moved from being a garden vegetable to a staple crop in Ireland for both human beings and animals since it was easy and cheap to cultivate potatoes. The Irish realized that they were able to grow potatoes even in the smallest patch in their garden.

Since potatoes are rich in minerals and vitamins, the poor consumed it in large quantities. They no longer had to depend on grains to obtain nutrition. This dependence on potatoes led to the Potato Famine in Ireland. The first time there was a famine was in the year 1739 when the weather was too cold to cultivate the crop. This episode did not have a significant impact on the Irish. However, the famine between 1845 and 1849, caused by a disease that rapidly wiped out all potato crops, led to the death of 1,000,000 Irish. Some Irish who survived either emigrated to the UK or US, while the others were left behind.

However, potatoes still remain a basic food item at every meal in Ireland. Potatoes are cooked with their skins intact. The skin is only removed at the table. The Irish believe that cooking the potatoes with their skin ensures that more nutrients remain in the potato.

Food in Ireland Today

Most cities in Ireland have a modern food culture and house multiple fast-food chains and ethnic restaurants. Some of the younger chefs in Ireland have embraced their heritage and culture and work with traditional Irish recipes. However, outside these cities, traditional Irish recipes are passed down from one generation to the next and families everywhere across Ireland cherish these recipes.

Meat

The Irish domesticated pigs for decades and maybe even centuries. This meat appears in multiple traditional Irish recipes either as sausages, bacon or gammon. Bacon and sausages and potatoes, of course, are commonly used ingredients in Irish cooking. The Irish also cook with beef and every household on St. Patrick's Day will have corned beef or Gaelic steak at its table.

Seafood and Fish

Ireland has many rivers and lakes and is surrounded by the sea. Therefore, seafood and dishes containing it play an important part in Irish cooking. Crab, oysters, lobster, cockles, white fish, fresh, smoked salmon and mussels are found easily and enjoyed by every family.

If you are intrigued by Irish cuisine, you have picked up the right book. This book covers some of the best Irish recipes, both modern and traditional, that will blow your mind. The directions given under each recipe will help you make the best version of an Irish meal.

Thanks again for purchasing this book. I hope you enjoy it!

Chapter One: Irish Baking Recipes

Irish Whiskey and Stout Chocolate Cake

Makes: 1 small cake

Ingredients:

For stout chocolate cake:

- ½ cup stout beer
- ¼ cup cocoa powder, unsweetened
- 1 large egg
- ½ teaspoon pure vanilla extract
- ½ teaspoon baking soda
- ¾ teaspoon baking powder
- 1/8 teaspoon fine sea salt
- 5 tablespoons unsalted butter
- 1 cup granulated sugar
- 6 tablespoons nonfat plain yogurt
- 1 cup + 2 tablespoons all-purpose flour

For whisky simple syrup:

- 2 tablespoons sugar
- 2 tablespoons water
- 2 tablespoons Irish whiskey

For whiskey cream frosting:

- 6 tablespoons unsalted butter, softened
- 1 cup powdered sugar, sifted
- ½ tablespoon caramel sauce (optional)
- ½ pound cream cheese
- 1 ½ tablespoons brown sugar, packed

- 1 ½ tablespoons Irish whiskey

For chocolate glaze:

- 2 ounce dark chocolate, chopped
- 1 tablespoon light corn syrup
- ½ tablespoon unsalted butter
- ¼ cup heavy cream

Method:

1. To make stout chocolate cake: Grease 2 small cake pans (of about 4-5 inches diameter) with a little butter. Place parchment paper in the pans.
2. Add beer and butter into a saucepan. Place the saucepan over medium heat. When the butter melts, turn off the heat and add sugar and cocoa and mix until sugar is dissolved completely.
3. Add egg and beat until well combined. Add vanilla and stir.
4. Add flour, baking soda, baking powder and salt into another bowl and stir.
5. Add a little of this mixture and a little yogurt into the butter mixture. Mix well.
6. Repeat the previous step until all of the flour mixture and yogurt is added.
7. Pour the batter equally among the cake pans.
8. Bake in a preheated oven at 350° F for about 35-40 minutes or a toothpick, when inserted in the center, comes out clean.
9. Cool for a few minutes in the pan before unmolding. Place on a wire rack to cool completely.
10. Meanwhile, make the whiskey simple syrup as follows: Add water and sugar into a small pan. Place

the pan over medium heat and stir. When sugar dissolves completely, turn off the heat. Cool completely.

11. Transfer into a small bowl. Chill until use.
12. To make whiskey cream cheese frosting: Fit the stand mixer with a paddle attachment. Add cream cheese into the mixing bowl and beat until creamy.
13. Add butter and beat until well combined.
14. Set the mixer on low speed and add in the brown sugar and powdered sugar.
15. Stir in the whisky and caramel and mix until well combined.
16. To make chocolate glaze: Add chocolate, corn syrup and butter into a bowl. Set aside.
17. Add heavy cream into a saucepan. Place the saucepan over medium heat.
18. When the cream begins to boil, turn off the heat and pour into the bowl of chocolate. Place a sheet of plastic wrap over the bowl to cover it. Do not stir or move the bowl for 2 minutes.
19. Stir until smooth. Do not stir or move the bowl for 2 minutes.
20. To assemble the cake: Cut each cake horizontally in the center of the cake. You will be left with 4 pieces of cake (This is a layered cake).
21. Place one layer of the cake on a cake stand.
22. Mix together simple syrup and whiskey in a bowl.
23. Brush the simple syrup mixture over the cake.
24. Spread about ¼ of the frosting (about 3-4 tablespoons) over the cake. Spread it with a leveler or a long serrated knife.
25. Place the next layer of cake.

26. Follow steps 22-25 until all the cake is used (you should be left with some frosting for the side). Crumb coat the topmost layer of the cake with frosting.
27. Chill for 15 minutes. Spread remaining frosting on the sides of the cake.
28. Chill for 10-15 minutes.
29. Pour chocolate glaze on top. Do not disturb the glaze and allow it to drip on its own.
30. Chill until use.
31. Slice and serve.

Spiced Apple Tart

Serves: 2-3

Ingredients:

- 4 ounces cream flour
- 1 ounce Irish butter
- ½ pound cooking apples, peeled, cored, cut into thick slices
- ½ teaspoon ground mixed spice
- A pinch of salt
- 1 ounce lard
- 1 ounce Demerara sugar

Method:

1. Pass flour and salt through a strainer into a bowl. Add Irish butter and lard and rub it into the mixture.
2. Pour enough cold water to make stiff dough.
3. Dust your countertop with a little flour. Place the dough on it and roll with a rolling pin.
4. Use half of the rolled dough and place in a small pie plate. Press it onto the bottom as well as the sides of the pie plate.
5. Meanwhile, add apples into a bowl. Sprinkle sugar and mixed spices over the apples. Toss well. Spread it in the pie plate over the dough. Sprinkle a tablespoon of water over the apples.
6. Cover the pie with remaining half of the rolled dough. Press both the edges of the rounds together. Make a couple of cuts on the cover.
7. Bake in a preheated oven at 350° F for about 25-30 minutes or golden brown in color.

8. Serve hot, warm or cold.

Cornflakes and Oat Cookies

Serves: 24-25

Ingredients:

- 2 large eggs
- 9.2 ounces brown sugar
- 8.5 ounces butter, softened
- 3.5 ounces sugar
- 9.2 ounces plain flour
- 3.5 ounces corn flakes
- 7 ounces oats
- 10.5 ounces chocolate chips
- 3.5 ounces dried cranberries or raisins (optional)
- 1 teaspoon baking powder
- 2 teaspoons baking soda
- 4 teaspoons vanilla extract

Method:

1. Add eggs, brown sugar, butter, sugar and vanilla into a large mixing bowl. Set the electric mixer on medium-high speed and beat until creamy.
2. Add flour, oats, salt, baking powder and baking soda into a bowl and stir.
3. Add into the bowl of eggs. Set the electric mixer on low speed and beat until just incorporated. Do not overbeat.
4. Stir in the chips, cranberries and cornflakes and continue beating on low speed until just incorporated. Do not overbeat.
5. Divide the mixture into 24-25 portions and shape into balls. Place on a plate. Press a few chocolate chips on

the cookies if desired. Cover the plate with plastic wrap. Chill for 2 hours.

6. Grease a baking sheet with cooking spray. Place the cookie balls on the baking sheet.

7. Bake in a preheated oven at 350° F for about 10-12 minutes.

Irish Barmbrack

Serves: 24

Ingredients:

- 5 cups chopped dried mixed fruit
- 5 cups flour
- 1 teaspoon ground nutmeg
- 2 eggs
- ½ cup lemon marmalade
- 3 cups hot brewed tea
- 2 teaspoons ground cinnamon
- 1 teaspoon baking soda
- 3 cups sugar
- 2 teaspoons orange zest, grated

Method:

1. Grease a large Bundt pan or 2 smaller Bundt pans with a little oil or butter. Set aside.
2. Place dried fruit into a bowl. Pour hot tea over it. Cover and set aside for 2 hours.
3. Drain off the tea. Squeeze the dried fruit lightly.
4. Add flour, nutmeg, cinnamon and baking soda into a bowl and stir.
5. Add eggs, marmalade and sugar into a mixing bowl. Beat with an electric mixer until sugar is dissolved. Add marmalade, soaked dried fruit and orange zest and stir.
6. Add flour and fold gently until just incorporated. Spoon the batter into the prepared pan.
7. Bake in a preheated oven at 350° F for about 60 minutes. To check if the cake is ready: When you press the top of the cake lightly, it should spring back.

8. Cool completely in the pan. Slice and serve.

Chapter Two: Irish Breakfast Recipes

Cheesy Hash Browns

Serves: 2

- 1 onion, chopped
- 2 potatoes, grated
- Irish cheddar cheese, grated
- 1 tablespoon oil

Method:

1. Place a large frying pan over medium heat.
2. Add oil. When the oil is heated, add potato and stir.
3. Add cheese and stir. Cook until cheese melts.
4. Divide into plates and serve.

Irish Eggs

Serves: 2

Ingredients:

- 1 tablespoon butter
- 1 small onion, minced
- 3 eggs, beaten
- 3 potatoes, peeled, sliced
- ½ green bell pepper, chopped

Method:

1. Place a skillet over medium heat. Add butter. When butter melts, add onion, potatoes and green pepper.
2. Cook until potatoes are brown.
3. Add eggs and cook until the eggs are cooked as the way you like it cooked.

Rhubarb Jam

Serves: 16

Ingredients:

- 1 ¼ pounds fresh rhubarb, chopped
- 1 teaspoon orange zest, grated
- ¼ cup water
- 1 cup white sugar
- 3 tablespoons orange juice

Method:

1. Add all the ingredients into a saucepan. Place the saucepan over medium low heat. Cook until thick. Stir occasionally. Cool for some time.
2. Sterilize canning jars and pour jam into jars. Fasten the lid.
3. Refrigerate until use.
4. Use with bread slices, muffins, etc.

Irish Toast

Serves: 3

Ingredients:

- ½ loaf French bread (8 ounces), cut into 6 slices
- ½ ounce Irish whiskey
- ½ teaspoon vanilla extract
- Confectioners' sugar to dust
- 2 large eggs
- ¾ ounce Irish cream liqueur
- 2 tablespoons butter + extra melted butter to brush

Method:

1. Add eggs, whisky, vanilla and cream liqueur into a bowl and whisk well.
2. Place a nonstick skillet over medium heat. Add a little of the butter. Let the butter melt.
3. Dip a slice of bread into the egg mixture and shake off excess egg. Place bread in the pan. Place 1-2 more slices of bread in the similar manner.
4. Cook until the underside is golden brown. Flip sides and cook the other side until golden brown.
5. Repeat steps 2-4 to make the remaining toasts.
6. Drizzle some melted butter over the toasts. Brush it evenly over the toasts. Dust with confectioners' sugar and serve.

Irish Bubble and Squeak

Serves: 8 (2 patties each)

Ingredients:

- 6 cups mashed potatoes
- 2 large eggs, beaten
- ¼ teaspoon freshly grated nutmeg (optional)
- All-purpose flour, as required, for dredging
- 8 cups cabbage, shredded cooked
- 2 cups cheddar cheese, grated
- Salt to taste
- Freshly ground pepper to taste
- Vegetable oil, as required, to fry

Method:

1. Add potatoes, cabbage, cheese, eggs, salt, pepper and nutmeg into a bowl and mix well.
2. Divide the mixture into 16 equal portions and shape into patties.
3. Place in the refrigerator for 60-70 minutes.
4. Place a small deep pan over medium heat. Add oil up to half. Let the oil heat.
5. Coat the patties with flour on both the sides by dredging in the flour.
6. When the oil is heated to 365° F fry the patties in batches until golden brown and crisp on the outside.
7. Remove with a slotted spoon and place over plates lined with paper towels.
8. Serve hot.

Corned Beef Hash

Serves: 2-3

Ingredients:

- 1 ½ tablespoons unsalted butter
- 1 ½ cups corned beef, finely chopped, cooked
- Salt to taste
- ½ cup onion, chopped
- 1 ½ cups potatoes, chopped, cooked
- Pepper powder to taste
- A handful fresh parsley, chopped
- Eggs, to serve

Method:

1. Place a small cast iron skillet (preferably) over medium heat. Add butter. When butter melts, add onion and sauté until translucent.
2. Add potatoes and corned beef and stir. Spread the mixture all over the pan.
3. Raise the heat to medium high heat.
4. Using a metal spatula, press the mixture on to the bottom of the pan. Let it remain in this position without stirring for a while, until the underside is golden brown. If you find the mixture is getting stuck to the pan then add some more butter.
5. Flip sides and repeat the previous step.
6. Sprinkle parsley, salt and pepper and stir.
7. Cook eggs either sunny side up or poached.
8. Serve eggs with hash.

Traditional Irish Porridge

Serves: 4

Ingredients:

<u>For porridge:</u>

- ½ cup oatmeal
- 2 cups water
- A pinch salt

<u>For topping:</u> Optional, use as required

- Milk
- Dark chocolate nibs
- Honey
- Nuts of your choice

Method:

1. Add all the ingredients into a heavy bottomed pan. Place the pan over medium heat. Stir constantly with a wooden spatula.
2. When it begins to thicken, lower the heat and simmer for 12-15 minutes or until smooth and thick.
3. Ladle into bowls. Serve with any of the optional toppings if desired.

Irish Breakfast Porridge

Serves: 2

Ingredients:

- ½ cup steel cut oats
- ¼ teaspoon salt
- 2 cups water

For topping: Optional, use any, as required

- Butter
- Cream
- Fruit of your choice
- Maple syrup
- Any other topping of your choice

Method:

1. Add oats and water into a heavy bottomed pan. Place the pan over medium heat. Stir constantly with a wooden spatula.
2. When it begins to thicken, lower the heat and simmer for 12-15 minutes or until smooth and thick. Add salt and stir.
3. Ladle into bowls. Serve with any of the optional toppings if desired.

Irish Steel Cut Oatmeal

Serves: 2

Ingredients:

- ½ cup steel cut oats
- 2 cups water
- 1/8 teaspoon ground cinnamon
- 2-3 walnut halves or almonds or cashews, chopped
- Milk to serve (optional)
- 1 small banana, sliced
- Brown sugar or honey to taste

Method:

1. Pour water into a heavy bottom pan. Place the pan over medium heat.
2. When water begins to boil, add oats and cinnamon and stir constantly until it starts to become thick.
3. Reduce the heat and cook for 15-20 minutes. Stir occasionally. Do not overcook.
4. Turn off the heat. Add milk if using, brown sugar, banana and nuts and stir.
5. Ladle into bowls and serve.

Chapter Three: Traditional Irish Drinks Recipes

Original Irish Cream

Serves: 8

Ingredients:

- ¾ cup + 2 tablespoons Irish whiskey
- 7 ounces canned sweetened condensed milk
- ½ cup heavy cream
- ½ teaspoon instant coffee granules
- ½ teaspoon almond extract
- ½ teaspoon vanilla extract
- 1 tablespoon chocolate syrup

Method:

1. Add all the ingredients into a blender and blend until smooth.
2. Pour into a container with a fitting lid. Fasten the lid.
3. Chill until use.
4. Shake well before pouring into glasses.

Frozen Grasshopper

Serves: 4

Ingredients:

- 1 ½ ounces crème de menthe, green
- 4 cups vanilla ice cream
- A handful fresh mint leaves, to garnish
- 1 ½ ounce white crème de cacao
- 8 ice cubes

Method:

1. Add crème de menthe, vanilla, crème de cacao and ice cubes into a blender.
2. Blend for 30-40 seconds or until smooth.
3. Pour into glasses. Top with mint leaves and serve.

Lime Sherbet Punch

Serves: ½ punch bowl

Ingredients:

- 4 cups 7-Up soda
- ½ quart lime sherbet

Method:

1. Add 7 –Up into a punch bowl.
2. Scoop out lime sherbet and add into the bowl.
3. Serve.

Irish whiskey Maid with Jameson

Serves: 2

Ingredients:

- 4 ounces Jameson Black Barrel Whiskey
- 1.5 ounces simple syrup
- 4 fresh mint leaves to garnish
- 2 slices cucumber to garnish
- 6 slices Japanese cucumber, muddled
- 2 ounces lime juice

Method:

1. Add half the whiskey, half the simple syrup, half the lime juice and 3 slices Japanese cucumber into a shaker glass. Muddle with a muddler.
2. Add crushed ice. Fasten the lid and shake until well combined.
3. Pour into a glass. Place 2 mint leaves and a slice of cucumber in the glass and serve.
4. Repeat steps 1-2 to make the other serving.

Figs and Sage

Serves: 2

Ingredients:

- 1 ounce lemon juice
- 1.5 ounce East India sherry
- 2 fresh sage leaves
- 1 ounce fig syrup
- 3 ounces bourbon
- Bolivian pink salt to garnish

Method:

1. Add lemon juice, East India sherry, sage leaves, fig syrup and bourbon into a shaker.
2. Fasten the lid and shake until well combined.
3. Place crushed ice into 2 glasses. Strain the mixture into the glasses.
4. Sprinkle Bolivian pink salt on top and serve.

Kale St. Patrick's Day Cocktail

Serves: 2

Ingredients:

- 2 ounces kale juice
- 1 ounce cucumber juice
- ½ ounce simple syrup
- 3 ounces tequila Blanco
- 1.5 ounces ginger beer
- 1 ounce fresh lemon juice

Method:

1. Add kale juice, cucumber juice, simple syrup, tequila Blanco, ginger beer and lemon juice into a shaker.
2. Add ice. Fasten the lid and shake until well combined.
3. Pour into 2 glasses.
4. Sprinkle Bolivian pink salt on top and serve.

Saint Casa

Serves: 2

Ingredients:

- 3 ounces Casamigos Anejo
- ½ ounce agave nectar
- 1 ounce Crème de Mure
- Guinness beer to top off
- 4 fresh blackberries
- Edible gold and green glitter to sprinkle

Method:

1. Add Casamigos Anejo, agave nectar and Crème de Mure into a shaker.
2. Add ice. Fasten the lid and shake until well combined.
3. Pour into 2 glasses.
4. Top off with beer.
5. Take 2 toothpicks and fix 2 blackberries on each. Sprinkle edible gold and green glitter on top.
6. Garnish with a blackberry skewer in each glass and serve.

Irish Old Fashioned

Serves: 2

Ingredients:

- ½ ounce honey syrup (mix together 2 parts honey and 2 parts water and chill)
- 4 ounce Redbreast Irish whiskey
- 4 dashes Angostura bitters
- Lemon slices to garnish

Method:

1. Add all the ingredients into a jug and stir.
2. Add lots of ice and stir until well chilled. Let it sit for a while until it dilutes a little.
3. Place ice in 2 old fashioned glasses. Strain into the glasses.
4. Garnish with a lemon slice each and serve.

Matcha Honey Spritzer

Serves: 2

Ingredients:

- ½ teaspoon matcha powder
- 2 tablespoons honey
- 2 teaspoons warm water
- Ice as required
- 4 ounces ginger ale
- 6 ounces dry white wine
- Lemon wedges to garnish

Method:

1. Add matcha powder and warm water into the shaker and stir until matcha powder dissolves.
2. Add honey and stir until well combined.
3. Add ice, dry white wine and ginger ale.
4. Fasten the lid and shake until well combined.
5. Pour into 2 glasses.
6. Garnish with lemon slices and serve.

Irish Buck

Serves: 2

Ingredients:

- 4 ounces Irish whiskey
- 6 ounces ginger ale
- Ice, as required
- 2 tablespoons fresh lime juice
- Lime wedges to serve

Method:

1. Take 2 glasses and fill it up with crushed ice.
2. Stir in the whiskey, ginger ale and lime juice.
3. Garnish with lime wedges and serve.

Fuzzy Leprechaun Cocktail

Serves: 2

Ingredients:

- 2 ounces peach schnapps
- 2 ounces vodka
- 1 ounce pineapple juice
- 2 ounces blue Curacao
- 1 ounce orange juice
- Ice as required
- 2 cherries to garnish
- 2 orange slices to garnish

Method:

1. Add all the ingredients into a shaker and shake vigorously until well combined.
2. Pour into 2 glasses. Garnish with a cherry and an orange slice and serve.

Irish Sour Apple Cocktail

Serves: 2

Ingredients:

- 2 ounces Jameson Irish whiskey
- 7 ounces Fever-Tree Elderflower tonic water
- Ice cubes, as required
- 3 ounces Smirnoff Sour apple vodka
- Green apple slices

Method:

1. Add Whiskey, vodka and ice cubes into a shaker and stir for a few seconds.
2. Fill 2 glasses with ice.
3. Strain the whiskey mixture into the glasses. Discard the strained ice.
4. Add 3.5 ounces tonic water into each glass.
5. Decorate with apple slices and serve.

Irish Iced Coffee

Serves: 2

Ingredients:

- 4 ounces Tullamore Dew Irish whiskey
- 4 teaspoons Demerara sugar
- Whipped cream, to serve
- 2 teaspoons ground espresso
- 6 ounces cold brewed coffee
- 4 teaspoons hot water

Method:

1. Add whiskey and espresso into a small bowl. Stir and set aside for 15-20 minutes.
2. Place a coffee filter over a cocktail shaker. Pass the whisky mixture through it.
3. Add sugar and water into a bowl and stir until sugar dissolves completely.
4. Pour into the shaker. Also, pour cold brewed coffee. Add ice to fill the shaker. Fasten the lid.
5. Shake vigorously until well combined and the outside of the shaker looks frosted.
6. Add ice into 2 glasses. Pour the cocktail into the glasses.
7. Garnish with whipped cream and serve.

Chapter Four: Traditional Irish Side Dish Recipes

Simply Rich Cheddar Scalloped Potatoes

Serves: 3-4

Ingredients:

- 3 cups potatoes, peeled, thinly sliced
- 1 small onion, chopped
- 1 cup cheddar cheese, shredded
- Salt to taste
- Black pepper powder to taste
- 2 tablespoons margarine, cut into thin slices
- ¼ cup half and half
- 1 cup milk
- 2 tablespoons flour

Method:

1. Place a skillet over medium heat. Add margarine. When it melts, add onion and sauté until translucent.
2. Add flour, salt and pepper and stir for a few seconds.
3. Stir in the milk and half and half. Stir constantly until thick. Remove from heat. Add ¾ cup cheddar cheese and mix until well combined.
4. Add potatoes and mix well. Transfer into a casserole dish. Cover the dish with foil.
5. Bake in a preheated oven at 350° F for about 30 -40 minutes or until the potatoes are tender. Uncover and

top with ¼ cup cheese or+ use more if you like it cheesy. Bake until the edges are light brown.

Irish Mushy Peas

Serves: 2-3

Ingredients:

- 4 ounces dried split marrowfat peas
- 1 ¾ cups boiling water
- Pepper powder to taste
- Butter, as required
- ¼ teaspoon baking soda
- Salt to taste
- A pinch sugar

Method:

1. Add peas into a bowl. Pour water over the peas. Add baking soda and stir. Let it soak for 7-8 hours.
2. Drain and add into a pot. Cover with water and place pot over medium heat.
3. When it begins to boil, lower the heat and cook until soft. When soft, drain the excess water.
4. Add salt, pepper, butter and sugar and stir. Mash lightly and serve.

Scalloped Cabbage

Serves: 3

Ingredients:

- 1 medium head cabbage, cut into
- Salt to taste
- 6 tablespoons milk
- ¼ cup + 2 tablespoons margarine
- ½ package club crackers, crushed
- ½ cup cold water
- 4 teaspoons flour
- Pepper powder to taste
- ¼ pound Velveeta cheese

Method:

1. Place cabbage in a bowl. Add a little salt and stir.
2. Add cold water.
3. Place a skillet over medium heat. Add ¼ cup margarine. When it melts, stir in the flour and whisk for 10-15 seconds.
4. Pour milk and stir constantly until thick. Stir in the cheese. Cook until it melts.
5. Place cabbage in a baking dish. Season with salt and pepper. Spread the cheese sauce over the cabbage.
6. Add cracker into a bowl. Melt 2 tablespoons margarine and add into the bowl. Mix well.
7. Sprinkle the crackers over the sauce.
8. Bake in a preheated oven at 350° F for about 30 -40 minutes or until golden brown on top.

Chapter Five: Traditional Irish Appetizer Recipes

Smoked Salmon on Irish Soda Bread Crostini

Serves: 3

Ingredients:

- 6 slices Irish soda bread, toasted
- ¼ cup butter
- 4 ounces smoked salmon
- ½ tablespoon chives, chopped
- 1 teaspoon fresh dill, chopped, to garnish

Method:

1. Add butter and chives into a bowl and stir.
2. Spread the mixture on one side of each slice of bread.
3. Spread salmon over each. Garnish with dill.
4. Cut into desired shape and serve.

St. Patrick's Day Deviled Eggs

Serves: 6

Ingredients:

- 6 eggs
- 2 tablespoons mayonnaise
- 4 drops green food coloring
- Green egg dye
- 1 small stalk celery from heart, minced
- 12 small parsley leaves

Method:

1. Add eggs into a saucepan. Cover with water. Place the saucepan over medium heat.
2. When it begins to boil, turn off the heat. Let the eggs remain in the saucepan for 15 minutes.
3. Drain the water and add cold water into the bowl. Place the bowl in the refrigerator for 30 minutes.
4. Make the egg dye following the instructions on the package. Carefully crack the eggs but do not peel. Each egg should be cracked at different spots so that the dye can get in through the cracks.
5. Now dip the eggs in the green dye for about 5 minutes.
6. Rinse and peel the eggs now. Cut into 2 halves lengthwise.
7. Carefully remove the egg yolks and place in a bowl. Mash the yolks and add celery, mayonnaise and green food coloring.
8. Fill the yolk mixture in the cavity of the eggs.
9. Garnish each half with a leaf of parsley and serve.

Cheese Dip

Serves: 5

Ingredients:

- ¾ cup Irish cheddar cheese, shredded
- ¼ cup green onion, finely chopped
- 1 teaspoon prepared horseradish
- ½ cup plain yogurt
- 2 tablespoons mayonnaise
- ½ teaspoon ground pepper

Method:

1. Add all the ingredients into a bowl and mix well. Chill and serve.

Pistachio Twists

Serves: 20

Ingredients:

- ½ package (from a 17.5 ounces package) frozen puff pastry sheets, thawed
- ¼ cup pistachio nuts, finely chopped
- 4 egg yolks
- 2/3 cup sugar
- 2 tablespoons water
- 4 tablespoons butter or margarine, melted
- 1 teaspoon ground cardamom
- 1 teaspoon ground cinnamon
- Flour, to dust

Method:

1. Place a sheet of parchment paper on a baking sheet. Use 2 baking sheets if desired.
2. Beat together yolk and water in a small bowl.
3. Dust your countertop with a little flour. Place a sheet of puff pastry over it and roll each until it is a square for about 9 inches. Take another sheet and repeat the same process.
4. Brush the sheets with egg yolk mixture. Sprinkle half the sugar over the sheets. Sprinkle half the pistachio nuts on one sheet. Do not sprinkle sugar or pistachio nuts along the border of the pastry sheets (about ¼ inch).
5. Cover the sheet (with pistachio) with the other sheet (that has only sugar on it), the sugar side facing down. Press the edges to seal.

6. Brush 2 tablespoons melted butter on top of the pastry. Cut into strips of about ¾ inch width.
7. Take a pistachio strip and twist it thrice. Repeat with all the strips. Place on the prepared baking sheet. Leave a gap of 2 inches between 2 twists.
8. Repeat steps 3-7 with the remaining 2 puff pastry sheets.
9. Bake in a preheated oven at 350° F for about 20 minutes or until golden brown on top.
10. Remove the baking sheet from the oven immediately and place on a wire rack to cool completely. Serve.
11. Store leftovers in an airtight container.
12. To serve: Reheat in an oven for 5 minutes and serve.

Avocado Bacon Pinwheels

Serves: 12-15

Ingredients:

- 4 ripe avocadoes, mashed
- 4 tablespoons lime juice
- 1 cup cilantro, chopped
- Salt and pepper to taste
- 6 tablespoons Greek yogurt
- 4 cups cooked chicken, diced
- 1 cup bacon, chopped
- 4 cups Kerrygold Aged cheddar cheese, shredded
- 12 tortillas (8 inches each)

Method:

1. Spread the tortillas on your countertop.
2. Mix together rest of the ingredients and spread over the tortillas. Roll the tortillas tightly. Place on a tray, with its seam side facing down. Refrigerate for an hour.
3. Chop into ¼ inch thick slices and serve.

Chapter Six: Irish Lunch Recipes

Irish Zucchini and Potato Pancakes

Serves: 12

Ingredients:

- 2 cups prepared mashed potatoes
- ½ cup milk
- 6 tablespoons unsalted butter
- 3 cups Yukon gold potatoes, shredded
- 2 small zucchinis, shredded
- 2 cups all-purpose flour
- 2 eggs
- 3-4 teaspoons fine sea salt or to taste
- 2 cups cheddar cheese, shredded
- Canola oil to make pancakes, as required

Method:

1. Add mashed potatoes, milk, salt, flour, eggs and butter into a bowl and whisk well.
2. Stir in the shredded potatoes, zucchini and cheddar cheese and mix well.
3. Place a large nonstick pan or griddle over medium heat. When the pan is heated, add 1-2 tablespoons oil. When oil is heated, place about 2 tablespoons of the potato mixture on the pan. Spread it until it is ¼ inch thick. You can make 2-3 more pancakes simultaneously.

4. Cook until the underside is golden brown. Flip sides and cook the other side too.
5. Remove and place on a baking sheet. Place the baking sheet in the oven to keep warm.
6. Repeat the above 3 steps and make the remaining pancakes.

Irish Pub Salad

Serves: 4

Ingredients:

- 1 cup mayonnaise
- 4 teaspoons fresh tarragon, chopped or 1 ½ teaspoons dried tarragon
- 5-6 teaspoons water
- 1 cup pickled beets, chopped
- 1 cucumber, sliced
- 2 tomatoes, chopped
- 1 cup celery, chopped
- 1 cup onion, sliced
- 3 cups cabbage, shredded
- 8 cups torn Boston lettuce or Bibb lettuce
- 8 ounces cheddar cheese or blue cheese, cut into wedges
- 4 hardboiled eggs, peeled, chopped
- 4 tablespoons malt vinegar or white wine vinegar
- 2 teaspoons whole grain Dijon mustard
- Salt to taste
- Pepper powder to taste

Method:

1. Add mayonnaise, tarragon, vinegar and Dijon mustard into a bowl. Mix until well combined.
2. Add water, salt and pepper and mix well. The dressing should be of dropping consistency.
3. Spread the lettuce leaves on a large serving platter.
4. Place rest of the vegetables in whatever manner you like to decorate, over the lettuce.

5. Place egg slices right on top. Pour the dressing all over the salad.
6. Scatter the cheese wedges and serve.

Irish Flag Salad

Serves: 2

Ingredients:

For salad:

- 3 ounces fresh baby spinach
- 1 medium orange, peeled, separated into segments, deseeded
- 1 tablespoon pistachio nuts, chopped
- 1 medium pear, thinly sliced
- 1 tablespoon crumbled feta cheese

For dressing:

- 1 ½ tablespoons canola oil
- 2 teaspoons lemon juice
- ¼ teaspoon orange zest, grated
- 1 tablespoon orange juice
- ½ teaspoon honey
- Salt to taste

Method:

1. Spread the spinach equally between 2 plates.
2. Divide and place pear slices, orange, cheese and pistachio over the spinach.
3. Add all the ingredients of dressing into a bowl and whisk well.
4. Pour over the salad.
5. Serve.

Green Salad

Serves: 2

Ingredients:

For salad:

- 3 cups greens of your choice (you can use a mixture of greens if desired)
- 6-8 spears asparagus, trimmed or asparagus tips, trimmed
- 1 ounce Irish cheddar cheese, chopped into small pieces
- 1 large green bell pepper, chopped
- 1 small Granny Smith apple, cored, chopped, tossed with a little lemon juice
- 1 tablespoon mint leaves, minced
- ½ small parsnip or ½ small carrot, grated
- 2 tablespoons raisins

For dressing:

- ¼ cup whole milk buttermilk
- 1-2 tablespoons apple cider vinegar
- Salt to taste
- A little cream for thinning (optional)
- 1 tablespoon sour cream of plain yogurt
- Pepper powder to taste

Method:

1. To make dressing: Add all the ingredients of dressing into a bowl and whisk well.

2. Add greens asparagus, cheddar cheese, apple, bell pepper, mint leaves and parsnips into a bowl and toss well.
3. Divide into 2 plates. Sprinkle raisins on top. Drizzle the dressing over it and serve.

Irish Dubliner Salad

Serves:

Ingredients:

- 2 heads butter lettuce, rinsed, spun dried, coarsely chopped
- 10-12 ounces Irish Dubliner cheese, grated
- 2 carrots, thinly sliced or grated
- A handful fresh herbs of your choice, minced
- 16 ounces pickled red beets, grated or raw beets, grated
- 1 ½ cups English cucumber, thinly sliced
- 2 cups red cabbage, shredded

For vinaigrette:

- 2/3-cup salad oil (sunflower, grape seed, safflower, etc.)
- 6 tablespoons white vinegar
- 4 teaspoons Irish mustard
- Salt to taste
- Pepper powder to taste

Method:

1. To make vinaigrette: Add all the ingredients of vinaigrette into a bowl and whisk well. Cover and set aside for a while.
2. Place lettuce leaves in a large, shallow bowl.
3. Place rest of the salad ingredients over the lettuce in any manner you desire.
4. Pour dressing on top and serve.

Saint Paddy's Irish Sandwich

Serves: 3

Ingredients:

- 1 ½ pounds corned beef brisket with spice packet
- ½ tablespoon balsamic vinegar
- ¼ teaspoon salt
- 1 small head cabbage, cored, thinly sliced
- 6 slices sourdough bread, lightly toasted
- 1 tablespoon olive oil
- ½ tablespoon spicy brown mustard + extra to spread on the bread slices
- Pepper powder to taste

Method:

1. Add corned beef into a pot. Pour enough water to cover. Stir in the spice packet. Cover with lid.
2. When it begins to boil, lower the heat and simmer until tender. It should take 50 minutes for every pound of meat to cook. Remove meat from the pot and place on your cutting board. Discard the water in the pot.
3. When cool enough to handle, cut into slices across the grain.
4. Add oil, mustard, vinegar, pepper and salt into a bowl and whisk well.
5. Add cabbage and toss well.
6. Spread mustard on 3 of the bread slices. Top with cabbage and corned beef. Cover with the remaining 3 bread slices.
7. Cut into desired shape and serve.

Leftover Corned Beef Sandwich

Serves: 4

Ingredients:

- 4 small ciabatta, halved, horizontally
- 4 ounces provolone cheese, deli sliced
- 12 ounces leftover corned beef

Method:

1. Place corned beef on the bottom halves of the ciabatta.
2. Place cheese slices over it.
3. Place in the toaster oven and heat for a few minutes until cheese melts.
4. Cover sandwiches with the top half of ciabatta and bake for a few minutes until the sandwiches are warm.
5. Cut into desired shape and serve.

Irish Potato and Leek Soup

Serves: 8-10

Ingredients:

- 4 teaspoons vegetable oil
- 4 stalks celery, chopped
- 4 cloves garlic, minced
- 8 cups vegetable stock or water
- 1 teaspoon pepper powder
- 3 cups light cream
- 4 teaspoons fresh dill, chopped
- 4 teaspoons fresh parsley, chopped
- 4 teaspoons fresh tarragon, chopped
- 4 cups leeks, chopped
- 2 small onions, chopped
- 8 medium potatoes, peeled, coarsely chopped
- 2 teaspoons salt
- 1 teaspoon dried thyme

Method:

1. Place a soup pot over medium heat. Add oil. When the oil is heated, add leeks, onion, celery and garlic and sauté until soft.
2. Add stock, thyme, salt, pepper and potatoes. When it begins to boil, lower the heat and simmer until potatoes are tender.
3. Stir in the cream and all the fresh herbs. Stir occasionally. Let it simmer for a few minutes. Turn off the heat. Set aside for 10 minutes.
4. Ladle into soup bowls and serve with warm bread.

Chapter Seven: Traditional Irish Main Course Recipes

Colcannon Soup

Serves: 3

- ¾ pound boiling potatoes, peeled, cut into 1 inch cubes
- 1 cup cabbage, shredded
- ½ pound leeks, white and pale green parts only, chopped
- 2 ½ cups chicken stock
- Salt to taste
- White pepper powder to taste
- 2 tablespoons butter
- ½ cup + 2 tablespoons half and half
- A pinch ground nutmeg
- A handful parsley, chopped

Method:

1. Place a large saucepan over medium heat. Add butter. When butter melts, add cabbage, leeks and potatoes. Sauté for a minute. Cover with a lid and cook until just tender. Add stock and stir.
2. When the stock begins to boil, lower the heat and cover with a lid. Cook until soft.

3. Add salt, pepper and nutmeg. Stir until well combined. Turn off the heat. Cool for a while.
4. Transfer into a food processor and blend until smooth or blend with an immersion blender.
5. Pour it back into the saucepan. Heat thoroughly. Add half and half and stir.
6. Ladle into soup bowls and serve.

Irish Roasted Salmon

Serves: 2

Ingredients:

- 1 tablespoon honey
- 2 tablespoons Irish whiskey
- ¾ teaspoon lemon zest, grated
- Salt to taste
- Freshly ground pepper to taste
- 2 tablespoons cider vinegar
- 1 teaspoon fresh thyme
- 1 tablespoon vegetable oil
- 2 salmon fillets

Method:

1. Place salmon in a bowl. Add rest of the ingredients into another bowl and stir. Pour into the bowl of salmon. Marinate for 4-5 hours in the refrigerator.
2. Place a rack in the roasting pan. Place roasting pan in the oven.
3. Pull out the salmon from the bowl and place on the rack.
4. Bake in a preheated oven at 350° F for about 10-12 minutes. Baste once with the marinade.
5. Bake until golden brown and cooked through.

Irish Lasagna

Serves: 3-4

Ingredients:

- ½ pound real Irish minced beef
- 1 small egg, beaten
- ½ teaspoon mixture of dried basil, thyme and oregano
- 4 ounces mozzarella cheese, shredded
- 6 lasagna sheets
- ½ pint ricotta cheese
- 1 clove garlic, crushed
- 4 ounces spaghetti squash
- 6 tablespoons parmesan cheese

Method:

1. Place a skillet over medium heat. Add beef. Sauté until brown. Drain excess fat and set aside the meat.
2. Add ricotta, herbs, egg and half the mozzarella cheese into a bowl and mix well.
3. Spread a little spaghetti sauce on the bottom of a baking dish.
4. Place 2 lasagna sheets over it.
5. Spread 1/3 of the cheese mixture followed by 1/3 of the beef mixture.
6. Spread some spaghetti sauce over it.
7. Repeat steps 4-6 twice.
8. Sprinkle Parmesan cheese and remaining mozzarella cheese.
9. Cover the dish with foil.

10. Bake in a preheated oven at 350° F for about 30 minutes. Uncover and bake until top is brown.
11. Serve hot.

Stuffed Cabbage Rolls

Serves: 3

Ingredients:

- 1 medium head cabbage, cored
- 1 medium onion, chopped
- 2 ounces pork sausage
- ¼ teaspoon allspice
- 4 ounces canned tomato sauce
- ½ teaspoon salt
- ½ teaspoon dried thyme
- ½ tablespoon butter
- 6 ounces lean ground beef
- ½ cup white rice or ½ cup brown rice, cooked
- 14 ounces canned tomatoes, with its juice
- 3 ounces canned tomato paste
- ¼ teaspoon garlic salt
- Sour cream, as required

Method:

1. Place a pot with water over medium heat. Add the whole cabbage into it. Let it cook until slightly soft. (Soft enough for you to be able to separate the leaves). Drain the water.
2. When cool enough to handle, separate the leaves. Shake to drop off any water droplets. Set aside.
3. Place a skillet over medium heat. Add butter. When butter melts, add onions and sauté until golden brown.
4. Add half the sautéed onions into a bowl. Also add rice, allspice, beef and pork sausage.

5. Using your hands mix well.
6. Place the skillet with half the onions back over low heat. Add tomato paste, tomato sauce, tomatoes, salt, pepper, garlic salt and thyme and stir. Let it cook for 10-12 minutes. Turn off the heat.
7. Spread the cabbage leaves on your countertop. Place a little of the filling near the stem side. Roll the cabbage and place with its seam side facing down in a baking dish that is greased with a little butter.
8. Repeat with all the filling and leaves.
9. Pour the cooked sauce over the rolls.
10. Bake in a preheated oven at 350° F for about 50-60 minutes.
11. Drizzle sour cream on top and serve.

Irish Stout Chicken

Serves: 2-3

Ingredients:

- 1 tablespoon vegetable oil
- 1 large clove garlic, minced
- 3 carrots, peeled, chopped
- 1 small onion, chopped
- 2 pounds chicken, cut into pieces
- 1 parsnip, peeled, chopped
- Salt to taste
- Pepper to taste
- ½ teaspoon dried thyme
- 1/3 – ½ cup stout beer
- 1/3 cup frozen peas
- ¼ pound button mushrooms

Method:

1. Place a skillet over medium heat. Add oil. When the oil is heated, add onion and garlic and sauté until translucent.
2. Remove with a slotted spoon and place in a bowl.
3. Place the chicken pieces in the skillet, in a single layer. Cover with a lid. Cook until light brown on all the sides.
4. Add the cooked onions back into the skillet. Add parsnip, carrot, salt, pepper and thyme and stir.
5. Pour beer over the chicken. When it begins to boil, lower the heat and cover with a lid.
6. Simmer until chicken is cooked through.

7. Remove the lid and cook on high heat for a few minutes until the sauce is thickened.

Bacon and Cabbage Pies

Serves: 3

Ingredients:

- 3 tablespoons butter
- 1 carrot, peeled, finely chopped
- 1 medium onion, thinly sliced
- ½ head green cabbage, chopped
- ¾ cup hot chicken stock
- ¾ teaspoon English mustard
- 1 tablespoon plain flour + extra to dust
- Salt to taste
- Freshly ground pepper to taste
- 1/3 cup single cream
- 6 ounces frozen short crust pastry, thawed
- 1 pound bacon joint
- 1 small egg yolk

Method:

1. Place bacon in a pot. Cover with cold water. Place the pot over medium heat.
2. When it begins to boil, lower the heat and simmer until cooked through. Remove the bacon and set aside on a plate. Retain a little of the stock (about ½ cup) and discard the rest.
3. Place a pan over medium heat. Add 1-tablespoon butter. When butter melts, add onion and carrot and sauté until golden brown. Turn off the heat.
4. Place a saucepan over medium heat. Add remaining butter. When butter melts, add flour and stir constantly for about a minute.

5. Pour slowly the bacon stock stirring constantly until it thickens.
6. Lower the heat and let it cook for 2-3 minutes.
7. Add cream, salt, mustard and pepper and stir. Add bacon and cabbage and mix well. Turn off the heat.
8. Dust your countertop with flour. Place the pastry on the countertop and roll with a rolling pin. Make 3 rounds from the rolled pastry to line a mini pie pan and make 3 smaller rounds to cover the pies.
9. Place the bigger rounds in the mini pie pans. Place a little of the filling in each pan. Brush egg on the edges of the pastry. Cover with the smaller rounds.
10. Press the edges of both the rounds together to seal. Brush the top of the crust with egg.
11. Bake in a preheated oven at 350° F until the crust is golden brown.
12. Remove from the oven and cool for a few minutes before serving.

Vegetable Shepherd's Pie

Serves: 5-6

Ingredients:

For topping:

- 1 ½ pounds Yukon gold potatoes, with skin
- 1 ½ pounds russet potatoes, with skin
- Kosher salt to taste

For filling:

- ½ ounce dried porcini mushrooms
- 3 cloves garlic cloves
- 1 tablespoon garlic, chopped
- 2 ½ tablespoons olive oil, divided
- 1 tablespoon tomato paste
- 1 cup dry white wine
- 1 tablespoon cornstarch
- Freshly ground pepper to taste
- ½ cup frozen pearl onions, thawed, halved
- 1 cup mixed fresh mushrooms, chopped into bite size pieces
- 6 tablespoons brown or French green lentils
- ½ teaspoon kosher salt + extra to season
- 1 ½ cups onion, chopped
- 1 bay leaf
- 4 cups vegetable broth
- 1 tablespoon gluten free white miso or tamari soy sauce
- 6 cups mixed fall vegetables like carrot, squash, parsnip, etc.

- 1 sprig rosemary
- A handful mixed fresh herbs of your choice.

Method:

1. To make topping: Place a sheet of foil on a baking sheet. Place all the potatoes on the baking sheet.
2. Bake in a preheated oven at 450° F until cooked through. It may take 45-60 minutes.
3. Place the potatoes into a ricer and rice the potatoes. Place in a large bowl. Add butter and mix well.
4. Add milk and salt and stir. Cover and set aside.
5. To make filling: Place porcini in a bowl. Pour 1-2 cups hot water over it. Set aside for a while.
6. Meanwhile, make the lentils as follows: Add lentils, 1 clove garlic, 2 cups water and salt into a saucepan. Place the saucepan over medium heat.
7. When it begins to boil, lower the heat and simmer until soft. Do not overcook.
8. Drain excess water in the lentils and throw away the garlic clove.
9. To make sauce: Place a heavy pot over medium heat. Add 1-½ tablespoons of oil. When the oil is heated, add onions and sauté until light brown. Stir in the chopped garlic and sauté until fragrant.
10. Add tomato paste and cook for a couple of minutes.
11. Stir in the bay leaf and wine. Scrape the bottom of the pan to remove any browned bits that may be stuck. Add porcini into the pan along with the soaked water. Do not add any residue of the mushrooms.
12. Cook until the liquid in the pot is half its original quantity. Add broth and stir. Cook until the broth is half its original quantity.

13. Pass the mixture through a strainer into a saucepan. Place the saucepan over medium heat. When the mixture begins to boil, mix together a little water and cornstarch and add into the saucepan. Stir constantly until thick.
14. Add miso, salt and pepper and mix well.
15. Add vegetables, 2 cloves garlic, rosemary sprig and pearl onions into a bowl. Drizzle 1-tablespoon oil. Toss well. Transfer on to a rimmed baking sheet.
16. Bake in a preheated oven at 450° F until cooked through. Transfer into a bowl and add fresh mushrooms. Toss well.
17. Mash the garlic cloves and add into the cooked sauce. Throw off the rosemary sprig.
18. To assemble: Spread the lentils in a baking dish. Spread the vegetables over the lentils. Spread sauce over the vegetables. Top with potato mixture.
19. Bake in a preheated oven at 450° F until top is brown.
20. Remove from the oven. Cool for a few minutes and serve.

Chapter Eight: Traditional Irish Dessert Recipes

St. Patrick's Day Parfaits

Serves: 8

Ingredients:

- 2 boxes (3 ounces each, 4 servings each) Jell-O instant pistachio pudding mix
- 4 kiwifruits, peeled, thinly sliced
- 6 drops green food coloring
- 4 cups milk
- Cool whip, as required
- Green coarse sugar, to garnish

Method:

1. Make the pudding following the instructions on the package with milk. Place in the refrigerator until it sets.
2. Add green drops into the bowl of cool whip and stir.
3. Take 8 parfait glasses. Layer the pudding, cool whip and rest of the ingredients in the glasses in any manner you desire.
4. Garnish with green sugar and chill until use.

St. Patrick's Day Crispy Treats

Serves: 12

Ingredients:

- 3 cups Rice Krispies
- ¼ teaspoon vanilla extract
- 5 ounces mini marshmallows
- 2 tablespoons margarine
- Green food coloring, as required
- Gold chocolate coins, to garnish

Method:

1. Grease a baking dish with a little oil or butter.
2. Place a pan over low heat. Add margarine. When it melts, stir in the marshmallows. Keep stirring until the marshmallows are completely melted. Turn off the heat.
3. Stir in vanilla and food coloring.
4. Add rice Krispies into the pan and stir quickly until well combined.
5. Transfer into the prepared baking dish. Press it evenly on to the bottom of the baking pan using a spatula that is greased with a little butter. Let it cool completely.
6. Slice into bars. Top with gold chocolate coins on each bar and serve.

Chocolate Mint Candy (Fudge)

Serves: About 30-35

Ingredients:

- 6 ounces semi-sweet chocolate chips
- 1 teaspoon vanilla extract
- 1-2 teaspoons peppermint extract
- 7 ounces canned sweetened condensed milk, divided
- 3 ounces white candy coating
- 6 drops green food coloring

Method:

1. Place a heavy saucepan over medium heat. Add chocolate chips and ½ cup condensed milk. When the chocolate melts, turn off the heat. Stir frequently.
2. Add vanilla and mix well.
3. Line a small square pan with wax paper. Spread half the mixture into the pan. Place the pan in the refrigerator for 10 minutes or until set.
4. Meanwhile, place a saucepan over low heat. Add candy coating and remaining condensed milk and stir until the candy coating melts and the mixture is creamy.
5. Add green color and peppermint extract and stir until well combined.
6. Pour over the firm chocolate layer in the pan. Place in the refrigerator for a few hours until it sets.
7. Chop into 1 inch squares and serve.

Kiwifruit Lime Jell-O with Yogurt

Serves: 8

Ingredients:

- 2 packages lime Jell-O
- 4 cups ice cubes
- ½ cup plain yogurt + extra to garnish
- 2 cups kiwifruits, halved, thinly sliced
- 8 slices kiwifruit to garnish
- 2 cups boiling water

Method:

1. Add Jell-O powder into a bowl. Pour boiling water into it. Mix until well combined and dissolved completely.
2. Stir in the ice cubes. Keep stirring until it thickens. Discard any ice cubes that are remaining in the bowl.
3. Set aside 1 cup of the Jell-O in the refrigerator for 30 minutes. After 30 minutes add yogurt and stir. Beat on high speed until it is twice the original quantity.
4. Place the remaining Jell-O also in the refrigerator until it thickens slightly.
5. Add kiwifruits into this bowl and fold gently. Refrigerate until set.
6. Spoon into glasses.
7. Garnish with yogurt and a slice of kiwi and serve.

Conclusion

Thank you once again for choosing the book.

This book brings Ireland's rich culinary heritage to life. Most traditional Irish recipes are difficult to make since there is a lot of technique involved. It takes time for someone, even from Ireland, to master those techniques. But, this does not mean that you cannot make those dishes at home.

Over the course of the book, you will have learned how to make different traditional recipes easily. Follow the directions written under each recipe, and at the end of the process, you can serve a complete Irish traditional meal and surprise your friends and family.

I hope you enjoy the recipes mentioned in this book.

Finally, if you enjoyed this book, then I'd like to ask you for a favor. Will you be kind enough to leave a review for this book on Amazon? It would be greatly appreciated!

Thank you and good luck!

Other Books by Grizzly Publishing

"Jamaican Cookbook: Traditional Jamaican Recipes Made Easy"

https://www.amazon.com/dp/B07B68KL8D

"Brazilian Instant Pot Cookbook: Delicious Pressure Cooked Meals Made Fast and Easy"

https://www.amazon.com/dp/B078XBYP89

"Norwegian Cookbook: Traditional Scandinavian Recipes Made Easy"

https://www.amazon.com/dp/B079M2W223

"Casserole Cookbook: Delicious Casserole Recipes From Around The World"

https://www.amazon.com/dp/B07B6GV61Q

Made in the USA
Middletown, DE
20 December 2020

29337367R00126